CONFESSIONS OF A

CHAOS
WHISPERER

MY LIFE AS AN ORGANIZING GURU, BUSINESS OWNER, AND MOM

Sonya Weisshappel

A POST HILL PRESS BOOK
ISBN: 979-8-88845-572-2
ISBN (eBook): 979-8-88845-573-9

Confessions of a Chaos Whisperer:
My Life as an Organizing Guru, Business Owner, and Mom
© 2024 by Seriatim Inc.
All Rights Reserved

Cover and book design by Cecile Rothschild.

Post Hill Press
New York • Nashville
posthillpress.com

Published in the United States of America
1 2 3 4 5 6 7 8 9 10

For Mom and Dad

DISCLAIMER

Throughout this book, I have endeavored to recreate events, locations, and conversations based on my recollections. To protect the privacy of individuals involved, I have altered or withheld certain names and modified identifying characteristics or details, such as occupations or places of residence.

It is important to note that the information presented in this book is intended as a supplementary resource and should not serve as a substitute for proper training in fields such as organization, efficiency management, relocation coordination, caregiving, or mental health advocacy. Before attempting to apply the techniques and skills described herein, please ensure that you do not exceed your level of experience, aptitude, training, or personal comfort.

If you require assistance with a relocation, renovation, or home organizing project, I encourage you to seek professional support. Please visit www.seriatim.net for further guidance.

TABLE OF CONTENTS

"

The practice of *tonglen*—sending and receiving—is designed to awaken bodhichitta, to put us in touch with genuine noble heart. It is a practice of taking in pain and sending out pleasure and therefore completely turns around our well-established habit of doing just the opposite. Tonglen is a practice of creating space, ventilating the atmosphere of our lives so that people can breathe freely and relax.

Pema Chödrön, *When Things Fall Apart*

"

AUTHOR'S GREETING

I know stuff. Not like trivia or tidbits. *Stuff*—as in, objects. Things you can touch. Tangible household goods. Items on an inventory. That's my métier.

If you're still getting acquainted with the role of a professional organizer, keep going. It's a field that requires a detailed explanation, as many people are unfamiliar with its purpose and scope.

Professional organizers are driven by a genuine desire to help others reclaim their lives and create spaces that nurture their well-being. It is a calling rooted in compassion, understanding, and the belief that everyone deserves to live in an environment that supports their physical, mental, and emotional health.

By providing the tools, support, and guidance through life transitions such as a relocation, renovation, or senior downsizing move—or by simply decluttering one room— we may bring our clients one inch further toward a lasting change.

Many people live with a sense of unease, overwhelmed by clutter, disorganization, and chaos in their physical and mental spaces. They may have accepted their situation as the norm, not realizing the toll it takes on their overall quality of life. As a professional organizer, I have the privilege of stepping into their lives, gently introducing the concept of organizing, and showcasing the transformative power it holds.

It is a remarkable journey to guide people who may initially be resistant or unaware of the benefits of professional organizing. By truly seeing and hearing them, I aim to instill hope, restore dignity, and guide them toward a brighter and more fulfilling future.

The reward comes when clients experience a critical shift in their perspective. They begin to see the connection between their external environment and internal discord. As the weight of clutter lifts, they gain a newfound sense of clarity, freedom, and peace. They realize the desperation they had felt deep inside, and the transformation can become a catalyst for positive change in various aspects of their lives.

The topic of organizing gained significant attention in the early 2010s, largely due to the popular TV show *Hoarders*. While this program brought the concept of decluttering and organizing into the spotlight, it also spawned a wave of lesser-known reality TV personalities looking for fleeting moments of fame. Extreme organizing became the prime focus. Over the years, I've consciously chosen not to participate as a guest organizer-therapist in such ventures.

According to the Anxiety and Depression Association of America, hoarding is a disorder that is often associated with obsessive-compulsive personality disorder (OCPD), attention-deficit/hyperactivity disorder (ADHD), and even depression. It may also be associated with Prader-Willi syndrome (a genetic disorder), psychosis, or dementia.

What I find problematic—actually, unacceptable—about hoarding shows is their attempt to condense complex interventions, counseling, treatment, and the journey to recovery into brief, entertainment-driven episodes.

While these shows may be captivating and even addictive to watch, their methods are often oversimplified and can be counterproductive. Instead of providing genuine help and support to individuals with hoarding disorders, these shows exploit their struggles and hinder their path towards physical and mental well-being. The language and terminology used in the context of hoarding can also be vague and ever-changing. Thankfully, the understanding of organizing as a tool for promoting health and wellness is steadily growing.

Individuals who hoard compulsively are attempting to fill profound voids within their psyche. It is crucial to make them feel seen and heard, recognizing the underlying emotional complexities driving their behaviors. My approach as an organizer may differ from others; there are no tricks or secrets to my technique. From the beginning to the final stages of an organizing project, I approach my clients and their families with unwavering patience, genuine compassion, and utmost respect.

I take the time to listen attentively and create a space where clients feel comfortable opening up about their struggles, fears, and vulnerabilities. By fostering a non-judgmental environment, I encourage honest and transparent conversations that delve into the emotional aspects of their hoarding tendencies.

Rather than imposing rigid rules or attempting quick fixes, I collaborate closely with clients to develop personalized strategies that honor their unique experiences and needs. This method involves a gradual and sensitive approach, allowing individuals to navigate their journey at their own pace while offering guidance and support at every step.

My team and I remain steadfast companions throughout the organizing process, providing reassurance and understanding during moments of resistance. I strive to create a sense of trust and safety, empowering clients to confront the underlying issues contributing to their hoarding behaviors.

We work towards healing and transformation by addressing the psychological and emotional aspects alongside the physical clutter. It is about clearing spaces and helping individuals reclaim control over their lives, build healthier coping mechanisms, and cultivate a sense of cohesion.

I can guide them toward a more balanced and harmonious existence by recognizing and honoring their individual stories. My ultimate goal is to empower clients to create spaces that reflect their true selves.

Some may jest about my role as the "Organizer to the Stars." Yes, I've had the privilege of working with a few famous faces over the years. But in my eyes, they are no different from anyone else. Their possessions, like ours, carry meaning and hold particular sway over their emotions. We are all modern-day consumers, susceptible to collections that grow beyond our control.

Comparisons to Marie Kondo are inevitable. I want to go ahead and address that. I hold her in high regard. I've read her books and applaud her for starting a serious conversation about organizing, decluttering, and downsizing. Even so, I hope this book offers another perspective on the art form. I do it differently. I have trouble putting it into words, but I like the Scandinavian concept of *Döstädning* ("death cleaning"). I don't believe in throwing things away. That's not what I do. I believe in repurposing.

Cue the "pig story." Everyone on the Seriatim team knows about the famous pig since he exemplifies that one person's trash—or donation—is another's treasured possession. He's a bronze statue that belonged to a sweet old couple with a pied-à-terre on Manhattan's Upper East Side. They loved being New Yorkers but were getting too wobbly to walk around the neighborhood, and the taxi bills were piling up. So they decided to move near their kids and grandkids in Connecticut.

It was a fairly typical situation, nothing out of the ordinary. The wife was very particular with me during the sorting and prep process: her family's objects were valuable and had to be sold. She had carved mahogany Chippendale furniture, hand-woven carpets, Asian urns and vases—those kinds of things. Her appraisals were three decades old, but she was confident her items would garner a high price at auction. They didn't. She nearly gave her most valuable object to the donation facility: a little bronze piglet that had been sitting on her husband's desk as a paperweight.

They considered it a worthless trinket. When I picked it up, I turned it over and looked at the bottom to find an artist's signature. I refused to donate it and waited to show it to the appraiser, who agreed it should go to auction. There, it fetched over $30k. To quote E.B. White, it was "some pig."

I like to examine the broader issue of life transitions. We're all in a state of transition. Whether it's a new baby, the death of a parent, a high school or college graduation, a job transfer, or a home renovation, you're going through something *at this precise moment.*

Chances are you want to avoid talking about it or feeling your way through it. Most of my clients call me because they don't know where to begin. Trust me, that's the hardest part.

Picture your dream place—your ideal spot on earth, your perfect little room or nook. Which objects do you see going with you? When making those decisions and taking action, I'm your lady.

I cannot help you avoid the pain of learning the lessons that accompany life transitions. I've learned many lessons the hard way, but they have made me wiser, more thoughtful, and more kindhearted.

Rather than fearing chaos, I see it as an opportunity for growth and exploration. It challenges us to think outside the box, adapt to unexpected circumstances, and find beauty amid disorder. By embracing a little chaos, we can discover hidden potential, break free from rigidity, and invite a sense of adventure into our lives. It reminds us that perfection is not always necessary and that exceptional journeys frequently start on unpredictable and unexplored terrain.

PREFACE

4:56 a.m., July 30, 1984. I just turned fourteen.

Daddy's home, but he's in a coma. He's lying in a hospital bed in the bedroom with the blue carpet and the blue and white walls. Aunt Joanne, a registered nurse, says his breathing has changed and his lungs are filling with liquid. He's not going to make it through the night.

Mom and Joanne alternate saying prayers and singing "Amazing Grace." They even tried telling a joke or two but ended up yelling at Daddy for leaving us, pleading with him to stay. He'd been in and out of City Hospital (today it's called New York-Presbyterian), where they did a lot of experimental surgery. It hadn't made any difference. The lung cancer had progressed to his brain.

When he started becoming incontinent, we knew he wouldn't be able to go back to work. Sometime in late April, he lost the ability to feed himself, and Aunt Joanne came to stay with us. Daddy was thirty-nine years old.

I think I remember how I first heard Daddy was sick, but I'm not sure. I've blocked out many details. In 1983, we were still living in San Francisco. That year, Daddy's good friend and business partner, Joe Plumeri, had pulled off quite a coup overseeing American Express's acquisition of Shearson Loeb Rhoades. He called and asked Daddy to come to New York. Mom and I stayed home in San Francisco while Daddy lived in and out of hotels and rental apartments in Manhattan.

We flew to the East Coast almost every month to visit him and hunt for apartments. We looked at over three hundred units before we settled on one at the Majestic on Central Park West. It had been owned by the playwright Marsha Norman. My mom said it was hard to find a proper kitchen. Most New Yorkers eat out and have small, unused kitchens. That wasn't an option for my mom. That was the beginning of her career in real estate, but I'll get to that later.

I had to be interviewed by half a dozen private schools, which systematically put me through the wringer. They wanted to know what I wanted to do with my life and I didn't have the foggiest idea. My childhood in San Francisco was about my friends across the street, where we were going that day, and at whose house we were sleeping over on the weekend. What do I want to do for a career? What world problems do I want to solve? After three or four interrogations, I finally learned to say what they wanted to hear. I said I wanted to be a brain surgeon even though that wasn't true. It sounded like I was confident and driven and would be a model student. It must have worked because I started Columbia Grammar & Preparatory School that fall.

We closed on the apartment in July of 1983 and moved in that August. Renovation work soon followed. We lived in a hotel and then temporary housing. Meanwhile, Daddy's traveling back and forth from coast to coast. In September, I got called into the principal's office. They said my mom wouldn't be home that evening because my dad had a seizure in California. That's probably the first I heard of Daddy's illness, but I didn't know it would kill him. I felt so alone and was so thankful that I had two new friends, Claudia and Jamie, who helped me get through it. We've been close ever since.

Daddy worked in a glue factory in Brooksville, Ohio, outside of Cleveland, during high school. That place must have had asbestos or something. When he got sick, renovation work halted. We were still unpacking boxes when we hosted the whole family for Thanksgiving. Mom must have known it would be the last time we could all be together.

The four of us were in that unfinished bedroom for hours. At some point, I saw what seemed like a poof—a jellyfish, a cloud—rise out of Daddy's stomach and hover over him before it disappeared. "He's gone," I whispered. But he wasn't dead, not definitively. It took hours for his body to die.

That moment and image stuck with me whether or not I witnessed his spirit leave his body. Perhaps that was my way of processing the enormity of my father's passing; it's also possible that such an experience taught me to be closer or more attuned to things others aren't. There's you and me, our skins, what we see on the surface with our eyes, and then there's something else. There's always something else.

Some people call it "essence." It's what lives on, continues, and recycles—it doesn't matter what word you use or how you rationalize it. Let's say you meet someone for the first time, and they make you feel good; there could be a strong impression of a past life together, places and paths that have crisscrossed. That's all part of their essence, their aura, even if they're unaware of it or can't describe it.

At the time, though, all I could do was run. Run fast, run away out of that ugly room. I run down the hallway, out the front door, and push the elevator button to go up. I want to go to the top of our building where there's a glass solarium. You can see the roof of the Dakota there, and much of Central Park. My mom's best friend, Barbara "BB" Brine, has the only apartment up there, a tiny one-bedroom right off the elevator bank. I had spent many afternoons and evenings there. I wanted to be close to the sky. "But you aren't allowed up there before 9 a.m.," they'd say, "or after dusk."

The elevator door opened, and there was Conrad, the operator who worked nights until 8 a.m. Very kind yet stoic. Deep waters. I burst into tears when I saw him. "Daddy died. I want to go up." He nodded and took me up without argument. I must have been there an hour or more before he came and got me and brought me back downstairs. We never had keys to our apartments. I just went inside and climbed into my bed.

There were two twin beds in my bedroom. I saw Aunt Josephine asleep in the other bed when I woke up. She must have taken the first flight out of San Francisco when she heard that Daddy was dying. She's a fantastic traveler and was always there when my mom or Joanne needed her. The wake lasted several days. I remember walking into the Frank E. Campbell Funeral Chapel on the Upper East Side, going up the stairs, and seeing Daddy lying in the casket.

The room was full of people. Grandpa Weisshappel hugged me and sobbed, "One shouldn't have to bury his child!" He and Grandma Darcangelo got divorced before I was born, so they didn't talk to each other. That was the only time I ever saw them together. Aunt Josephine arranged to put "Sonia" roses at the foot of the coffin; they have a lovely orange-pink bloom. I later learned that they were hybridized in the same year as my birth, which was especially fitting.

The funeral was held at the Church of the Blessed Sacrament on West 71st Street. Mr. Plumeri gave the eulogy. I remember nothing except the long line of cars on the way to Gate of Heaven. And then that quiet, cloudy feeling of being home again. A teenager's life is dramatic and overwhelming and hormonal and awful to begin with. Add in the uncertainty of death and change—

significant change, like the world's been turned upside down. That was the feeling in our apartment, hovering over the space.

Objects that belonged to my father took on new meaning for me, new value and a strong sense of "speaking." I began to realize the ability to see and feel objects and their importance in people's lives. That's my superpower, my lightning rod, my singular language.

In college, I worked as a props mistress for the theatre department. I was good at it, too. I went on a shopping errand with my friend Tobin and spotted a table. I wasn't looking for a table but couldn't resist it. "This is such a fabulous table," I told him. "Look at this table!" I asked him to help me flip it over, and when we did, we discovered the word "Wiseapple" carved under the top. It was a "woah" moment for both of us. We didn't buy it, but I had such an energetic need to touch that table and figure out who made it and where. You don't usually feel the urge to look under large pieces of furniture, but I knew it was trying to say something to me, if not a simple "hello."

Years later, my mom and I were responsible for cleaning out Grandma Darcangelo's Florida condo after she passed away. She was very neat; there was hardly anything to do except go through the closets and donate her old clothes. I found a jacket that *screamed* at me. I had to put it on. The following day, I wore it to her funeral, and her girlfriends approached me at the church and said, "That was her favorite coat." I replied, "She told me to put it on."

Sonya Weisshappel

One of my favorite clients was a well-known child psychiatrist who dealt with families who had experienced trauma. She worked out of her brownstone in Brooklyn and had a terrific library and a playroom downstairs. When I arrived in the house to do an estimate, her assistant greeted me, escorted me inside, and kindly offered me a seat.

It was a big, blue chair, all sunken-in. As I sat down, I was physically rejected by it, as if it had sent me an electric shock. I yelped and shot back up. The assistant pointed out that the doctor sat in that chair when she listened to children's abuse stories. And I thought, OK, that makes sense. To someone else, it's an old chair in the middle of the room, not an antique, nothing special. But I know many years of fear, sadness, anger, and heartache have been collected and stored there.

Daddy came from a family of Midwestern, middle-class, blue-collar workers in the 1960s. He had a genuine work ethic and a positive, "broken-clock-is-right-twice-a-day" attitude. When he joined corporate America, he saw that he was rewarded for hard work. The harder he worked, the more money he made. He loved that. He loved that sense of balance. I remember him discussing the two sides of the equation and ensuring they matched. Daddy had a better brain for business than I do, but even he would admit that money isn't everything. Physical and mental health, community, respect for myself, my company, my family. And time. Now that's something I wish

Daddy could have bought for himself. I wish I could have given him that gift. If I can grant people more time without stress, more time to be together, and more time to heal, I'll work harder and harder for each new client who lets me in.

I see my father's numbers every day. On a business card or a subway advertisement, the address of a midtown office building, even the "lucky lotto" picks from the occasional fortune cookie. And indeed, like clockwork, when I look down at my watch: 4-5-6. That's how I know he's watching out for me.

This book is my exercise in healing.

CHAPTER 1

Curbing the Chaos

Disorganization knows no cultural, political, or geographic boundary. The need for organization is everywhere.

From as far back as elementary school, I felt that I was different. While some might dismiss these experiences as mere childhood quirks, I couldn't help but entertain the possibility that there was a genuine reason behind my uncommon perception of the world around me. It seemed as though three-dimensional objects had a voice that resonated with me.

In 1981, Dr. Richard Soghoian became a part of Columbia Grammar and Preparatory School, bringing with him a visionary mindset, contemporary thinking, and the esteemed authorship of the influential book *Mind the Gap*, which delved into the realm of academic leadership. He was one of the few teachers or administrators who got me. I was tested for learning disabilities and discovered I had dyslexia.

Confessions of a Chaos Whisperer

At last, something that made sense. It wasn't me; it wasn't my fault. Even though that disorder was taboo in the 1980s, especially in private school, I could craft a cubbyhole to hide in and learn about myself and my nature as an empath. I hadn't fully grasped it yet, but I had certain tendencies as a helper and healer.

I excelled at art history and ceramics classes taught by Ms. Price. She knew I was not fond of writing and encouraged me to create scrapbooks to sort out my thoughts. For one assignment, I browsed through dozens of magazines to find parallels to classical art in fashion and architecture. I discovered I could speak with images. Looking back on it, I see now that these were the earliest catalogs and inventories of my "organizer brain." I relished the task and the quiet time. To this day, I am a proud, prolific scrapbooker.

I also figured out I could organize the prom or do the yearbook layout because I saw how those things should be planned and executed. Instead of wallowing in woe-is-me, I showed them what I could do. And I learned that other people needed me to do these things. It gave me such a sense of purpose. The ability to get along with people and make friends quickly also played a role—I knew how to find the best in everyone and learn to observe them and figure out what they're good at even when others can't. Even now, I take on and can become exhausted by other people's suffering. To desensitize, I have to plan time for self-care—a lesson I've had to learn and relearn many times over.

Sonya Weisshappel

When I was a student at the University of Wisconsin at Madison, I spent my summers working on Atlantic Avenue in Brooklyn. My boss was a man named Bruce, who owned a big warehouse and imported European linens, mostly napkins and tablecloths. He had superb taste but was a terrible businessman and generally a nasty person. He was shaped like Jackie Gleason but had not one ounce of his humor.

He'd spend all day fuming about money and screaming at people over the phone. When he hired me, he told me I'd make calls and ask for collections. I didn't know I'd end up managing the office.

On any given day, we'd receive an order, import the fabric, and send it off to be customized according to the desired dimensions. All those people had to be managed and followed up with daily, if not hourly. For each order, Bruce had to figure out what inventory he had, what had already been sold, how much he had to charge for shipping, and what his cut would be. He was dreadful at it. I rode the subway train from 72nd Street to Borough Hall daily and walked through downtown Brooklyn. That neighborhood has all the French speakers, and great little bistros served baguettes with brie and butter on the side. New York is hot in the summer, but I didn't have to worry about wearing stuffy clothes and typing in some miserable office. It could have been worse.

Bruce gave me no guidance, no training, and no information. He told me to figure it out. He always shouted, "Rich people are only rich because they don't pay their bills!" He'd smash the phone on the receiver so hard that it broke the dial plate. His list of receivables was longer than the Dead Sea Scrolls, and he never got paid on time. I always wondered why he didn't ask for a fifty-percent deposit. By the end of that first summer, I was running his entire production line. He never said a kind word to me; he only pointed out something I'd done wrong. It was excruciating, but I learned much about inventory, management, and working with big-name stores and hotels. Macy's, Bloomingdale's, and Bergdorf's all bought from him, and I got to interact with worldly and sophisticated people who spoke Russian, Spanish, and German.

Back at school, I was dating a boy named Jeremy from the island of O'ahu. His parents were academics from the Midwest who established their teaching careers at the University of Hawai'i at Mānoa. After graduation, in the spring of 1992, we flew to Honolulu for three months to get summer jobs and make some money. Jeremy got a job at the local news station and loved it; I found work through an Atlantic Avenue friend who had connections in the export business.

Due to pesticides, or lack thereof, you can only sometimes export Hawai'ian fruits or vegetables to other countries; Germany was an exception. So I met this German importer fellow who shipped Hawai'ian fish, mangoes, and papayas via cargo planes that looked like something out of *The Temple of Doom*.

I handled the fruit. Truckloads of mangoes and papayas had to be put into boxes according to color and size.

You couldn't pair a teensy one with a ginormous one; it had to be uniform. But they're organic pieces of fruit; they're all different. I thought of it as a big puzzle, and I'm good at puzzles.

The German man mostly hired Koreans: men for the fish and women for fruit. Because I was the only English-speaking person on the team, I became the foreman of the production line. In the mornings, from 8 am until about 3 pm, I was responsible for sorting through and packing. There were about ten other women who helped me. Farmers would bring in shipments by truck. We lined up the crates and skids full of fruit and would sort through them, packing, labeling, and shipping out.

We packed hundreds of boxes a day. I soon learned everything there was to know about inventorying, packing, and shipping papayas and mangoes. I didn't realize it then, but this began my professional career. Someone was paying me to be an organizer and move manager!

Everyone looked out for each other and was genuinely kind. I picked up a few words in Korean while I sat with the other ladies in the shade, eating our lunches— often homemade kimchi. I even learned how to drive. In the afternoons, I'd go to the beach, grocery shop, or read a book. No children, no responsibilities. It sounds cliché when people say, "Oh, this is paradise!" But it was. Jeremy was happy as a clam being home and soon announced that he wanted to stay. I wasn't prepared to sort papayas and sleep in Jeremy's parent's house for the rest of my life. If we were full-time residents, I needed to find an apartment and something else to do. So I did. That's when I started working for Larry Kobata. He was my first real mentor.

The Kobatas were Japanese through and through: generous, well-mannered, and levelheaded. They had no children, so I became their adopted daughter. Larry worked with all the shopping malls in the archipelago and went to Siam and Guam a couple of times a year on buying trips. When he hired me, he was in an office space in Waikiki and was trying to shift to a bigger one in the same complex. He only had a month to get everything packed and ready to be redistributed. That was my first job as a move manager.

Larry had never had a good office manager. They had files and papers everywhere. And when I started, I said, "If I'm going to manage this move, I need to know where everything is and try to make sense of it." It was all paper-based; I wonder if they even had a computer. One evening, around 10 o'clock, Larry returned to the office after dinner, and I was still sitting there, taking apart his whole filing system. He said, "You need to go home, Sonya." I couldn't help myself. I loved taking everything apart and putting it back together again. I knew I had good instincts, but I needed practice. That's how I got good at organizing, good enough to know it was something I should be doing full-time.

Larry represented Fossil Group, less than ten years old and new to Hawai'i. He also distributed Whiting & Davis, those sensational metal mesh handbags and clutches.

Larry took me on a few trips to the showrooms to meet his sales reps. He'd fly me to and from New York to the Fossil showroom, Napier, or Ann Heckathorn's in midtown.

I was wholly engrossed in the business. I learned everything about managing inventory, merchandising, figuring out what skews were selling and what we needed to get rid of, how to separate it, and on which list or ledger to write it down. Should we send it back or sell it at a discount? Buy it from the store and then do a sample sale? I was asking all of these questions and more.

Two and a half years went by. Traveling to and from New York made me homesick. Hawai'i is beautiful, but people tended to work on what they call "island time." As a New Yorker, I had a drive and a work ethic and needed to feed off other people's energy. So I left my job, sold off the furniture, packed up my cat, Tommy, and flew back to the Big Apple.

We lived uptown with Mom. I didn't care for it and started to get antsy. I dreamed of working for National Geographic or anyone who produced nature videos. I even applied to work at museums with film departments and preservation centers. All of that fascinated me. One reasonably big thing always got in my way: putting together a resume and, worse yet, writing that pesky cover letter.

I liked reading for pleasure, but I hated reading assignments and doing research. And writing was never my forte (this book has had its fair share of agonizing moments). I had always found my work and gotten hired through conversations and meeting people. I prefer a handshake and a smile to a cold, sterile piece of paper mailed to some stranger. I craved personal contact. I'm a networker and a unifier. That's my magic. If I have to write something down, I feel ordinary; I'm exceptional if I can connect on the phone or in person. I had that instinct and knew it had to be more accessible.

I asked all my friends what I was good at and what I should do. The word "organized" kept popping up. "You're so organized," or "You are great at organizing." So I picked up the phone book and went to the O's. There were only three companies under "Organizer," and I called them all. One of them was a lady I'll call Ms. Y. We spoke on the phone, and she hired me on the spot. It was that simple. I had gotten my first job as a professional organizer.

At the time, Ms. Y was in her late 50s and ran the business out of her apartment in Rose Hill, near Baruch College. She later rented a tiny office space a few blocks away on Park Avenue. She was a tyrant who burned through people right and left. She'd scream like a banshee and make her employees—all independent contractors—wait three or four months before being paid. My first assignment was a sweet old man in the West Village who needed help with his kitchen cabinets. He opened the door and said, "Oh, I'm so happy you aren't that horrible woman!" I thought, *are you kidding me?* "I'm not here to make you feel bad," I replied. "I'm here to play. So let's play." It was like therapy for me—and I was being paid!

Ms. Y became president of the local chapter of the National Association of Productivity and Organizing Professionals (NAPO, but it should have been NAPOP!). Her brand was *the* brand because she was better at politics than being an organizer. She knew all the management companies and did everything she could to make the playing field uneven.

In the organizing world, Ms. Y was the Queen Bee. Or so she thought. Sure, it was lucrative (for her), but it was stagnant. We were stuck doing celebrity closets and kids' rooms. The clients were terrific—some of them award-winning actors and TV personalities—and I began to see missed opportunities. It hit me: people need to get organized because something's changing. They aim to have a baby, get married or divorced, downsize, move their elderly parent in or out, or sell and move to their country or beach house (or sell that, too!). Getting organized or "tidying up" is only the tip of the iceberg. More often than not, you're preparing for something more significant and complex—something that needs top-tier logistical planning to see it through to the next step.

I no longer wanted to be a contractor, feeling adrift, never knowing whether I had any control or say-so. I tried to plan relocations from the beginning and not parachute in at 8:45 am before a 9 am move. When I told her I wanted to meet with her connections in the relocation industry and work with their teams directly, she turned beet red. I thought she was going to breathe fire at me across the desk. After a moment, she said, "I'm the expert;

you're not. I pay more in taxes than you make in a year." I told her I wanted to leave and gave her six weeks' notice. She said that wasn't good enough; she needed six months to find a replacement. I was young and slightly foolish, so I reluctantly agreed.

Those months were unbearable. I'd go to sleep some nights and cry like I'd been punched. Ms. Y told me repeatedly that I'd never cut it as a business owner, that I wasn't smart or capable enough to achieve anything without her. My inner critic's response: *"Game on!"*

I always joke that Ms. Y taught me what I didn't want to be. I vowed that I'd never treat clients or employees like she did. Bruce taught me some of those lessons, too, and I think about them daily. Years later, I ran into Ms. Y at an organizing event in New Jersey. I approached her and said, "Nice to see you." She smiled at me and asked if I'd like to ride the ferry back to Manhattan. We chatted civilly. She told me her mom had recently died after a long illness. Ms. Y had never been married, had no children, and felt alone and probably more than a little scared. I never saw her again, but I think of her often and whisper a little thank-you for the lessons—both in business and life. She was tenacious, and her work meant everything to her. She was a pioneer with the courage and audacity to call herself an organizer when no one else was doing it.

I didn't start my own organizing company overnight. I didn't even begin looking for that kind of work immediately. Ms. Y had exhausted me, and I felt depleted but deliriously free. My brain was firing on all cylinders, and I wanted to try different things. One day, I talked to my mom's neighbor, Ms. Seltzer, who told me she knew a five-star producer who needed an intern. She said, "You're gonna love him!" Now, almost thirty years later, I'm proud to call him my husband.

CHAPTER 2

Panchali

She was born in Virginia, and her birth name was Jimmy Lu. She always joked about having gotten out of the trailer park. She was a classically trained singer, but she could sing anything—Broadway, song cycles, opera, you name it. She'd perform for anyone who'd listen. I think I heard her break a glass once. She enjoyed making people smile and laugh. She became a devotee of Swami Muktananda and changed her name to Panchali. Her yoga class, which she called "Fat Yoga," was open to anyone who wanted to learn to be more flexible, even if they were seniors sitting in chairs. After my wedding ceremony, I'll never forget her singing at Gotham Bar and Grill. No one present that day will likely forget it either.

When I first met Panchali, she lived near Lincoln Center, in a third-floor walk-up. She had recently finished touring a show and was preparing to rehearse a Rodgers and Hammerstein, her specialty. Mom first met her in the Bahamas at Sivananda Ashram Yoga Retreat. Mom was there with a girlfriend from high school, Mary, and they tittered like eight-year-old girls whenever they got together. They were all in little huts on the beach. When it came time for lights out, they couldn't control themselves. They must have been squealing with laughter. Panchali marched over to the door, knocked on it, and exclaimed, loudly yet mellifluously, "You two are having way too much fun. I want some!" The three of them became fast friends. Mom soon discovered that Panchali lived right around the corner in the city. She became part of our family.

Panchali had an impressive stage career. She was in the first revival of Zorba in 1983, the Joel Grey revival of *Cabaret* in 1987, and a thirty-city U.S. touring production of *Fiddler on the Roof* with Chaim Topol in 1989. Back home, she was in the Lincoln Center Theater's revival of *Show Boat* and the original *Ragtime*, which was unforgettable.

Panchali loved touring on the road because she could leave her chaotic life behind. When she was at home in New York, it was another matter entirely. I am trying to remember exactly how or why I started working with her. We were all sitting at the kitchen table in the Majestic, and I told her I had a talent for dealing with clutter, to which she responded, "Well—. I have a bit." She was a big personality, and it was a big job with even bigger lessons for me.

The first thing that comes to mind is the smell. As I walked up the staircase, I caught a whiff, and it only got stronger as I approached the front door. Some of it involved letting a little rescue Maltese, Cookie, urinate inside the apartment. Yet more challenging to pin down was the smell of dead mice, which followed her outside of the apartment now and then. Aside from that, the 500-square-foot space was stacked full. It was nearly impossible to maneuver around the piles of paper and objects. There was no order to anything; her brain sometimes switched off, and she'd drop things on the floor and walk away.

There was one spot on the sofa where she could sit and watch TV. I soon learned she was sleeping there, too, since her bed was full of dead mice. If you tried to move or adjust the furniture, a swarm of roaches would run out, up the wall, do a loop-de-loop, and dash back. I knew the sofa and other things had to leave the apartment to curb the infestation.

For five weeks, in May through June of 1996, I worked almost daily at Panchali's apartment on 67th Street. She paid me ten dollars an hour. I started in the bathroom and took out anything that didn't belong: shoes, dog bones, Chinese food containers (she never cooked at home), etc. I had to bring a change of clothes with me every time, strip down, put my work clothes in a plastic bag, and run home to wash them. Luggage was blocking the hallway that led to the kitchen. When I finally reached the refrigerator, I opened it, thinking it would be empty. I have yet to make that mistake twice.

Some days Panchali would be with me; others, she'd find a way to escape. When she was there, I got to know her better. We built a relationship by discussing India, traveling, food, and culture in general. She was academically gifted and read a great deal. She had studied music at Carnegie Mellon University and could hear language and mimic accents like you wouldn't believe.

She was fiendishly clever and could wordsmith anyone under the table. She was also quite tech-savvy and was a bona fide gadget geek. She had a computer, printer, scanner, the whole kit, and caboodle, all jumbled together—but that was hardly the worst part. Cable wires were even more prominent, thicker, and uglier than they are today and even more painful to organize.

It was during this time that a lightbulb flickered on in my brain. I started putting pieces of the puzzle together. It wasn't long before I realized that women who practiced Panchali's hoarding style had been victims of sexual abuse as children. I've returned to this topic repeatedly over the years, and my findings have been more or less consistent. I've always wanted to do a study alongside a research psychologist and install a simulated, interactive hoarding exhibit at a museum or gallery space. Perhaps that'll be book number two!

Panchali refused to accept or acknowledge it. One day, the eviction notice appeared on her door. The trash was piled so high you could no longer get through the front door without ramming it open with your shoulder. The super hovered over her, watching her every move like a hawk, waiting and hoping she'd leave as many of them do in New York. We had to act fast. We cherry-picked what she cared about and walked away from everything else. There was nothing of actual value.

Whenever we moved a big piece of furniture, we'd notice dried specks all over the floor, like kitty litter. We realized it was mouse droppings. We removed over a hundred trash bags to get to the good stuff. It was one of the few jobs I'd describe as a struggle.

Mom found her a new place nearby, on 65th Street across from Shun Lee West. One of my good friends from the New York Council of Relocation Professionals lived in that building. We orchestrated having shelves built and bars put up in the closets. We moved her out and in, paid the deposits, unpacked the boxes, and got everything set up. We even put a cover on the toilet seat. In the beginning, Panchali thrived. She joined Overeaters Anonymous and lost over 150 pounds. At one point, when she was at her thinnest, she was strong, healthy, and quit all of her medications. But I don't think she was ready for her new body's psychological toll on her. She got freaked out because men started to look at her. It triggered her, and she began eating again. It all fell apart at a rapid speed. For Panchali, things never reset back at square one—they went to negative five.

The familiar cycle started over again. Within a couple of years, the new building managers were after her, too.

Same deal as before: the smell, the roaches, the rodents. For all I know, some mice hitched a ride from the old apartment. Mom kept putting money in her account so she could buy dog food. She even came over and picked up her dry cleaning, laundry, and dishes. Then, in 2008, the whole world was in a financial crisis. Our family was affected like all the rest, and we didn't have as much money to spend on Panchali. She felt betrayed and didn't speak to us for months.

Like many women in the theatre, Panchali felt safer with gay men. That was her creative superpower crowd: musicians, dancers, composers, and conductors. She could talk to anyone about anything, spar with the wickedest of wits. She despised authority figures, especially if they were male, and wasn't shy about dishing out tongue lashings. But she could also speak to kids and tune into their wavelength like no one I've ever met.

Panchali's subliminal self was a young child. She'd sing and entertain people rather than take responsibility for her apartment or messes; she preferred getting her nails done to paying bills; she ignored eviction notices and blamed it all on the super or a landlord. But you couldn't say she was lazy or irresponsible—and certainly not uncaring. I understand now that there's a reason why she behaved like a big kid: Her childhood had been stolen from her. She grew up in poverty, abused by her stepfather; her mother was jealous and refused to help her, so it went on for years. Panchali confessed that a part of her knew it was wrong but was scared of him. Then there was a part of her that enjoyed it. It was oh so complicated and gave her a Gemini quality of inhabiting two modes of being, often simultaneously.

When I was pregnant with Bev, I got appendicitis. Mom was out of town, so I called Panchali. She showed up at the hospital *tout de suite*, singing, chanting, and praying all night. I believe those prayers saved my life: The doctors found cancer in my appendix that may have gone unnoticed and unattended. I think I got it from all the dust I inhaled on 9/11.

Panchali was also there when I went into labor a few months later. Mom was still out of town at a cousin's wedding, and Panchali came to my room at Lenox Hill. She sang and prayed, smiling big and waiting to hold Bev in her arms. She doted on and loved that baby almost as much as I did. It was the first family event Mom had ever missed, and I was so fortunate to have Panchali.

One would think there was enough affection stored away in the love bank. I was wrong. My final conversation with Panchali was horrendous. I had broken my ankle and was on painkillers around the clock. Mom had knee surgery one morning, and people were calling and texting me to find out how it went. As usual, I was running between appointments with fifteen minutes to spare. Mom sent me a picture of her knee from her hospital bed, all blue, black, and maroon. In hindsight, I know I should not have shared it in a group chat, but I made an executive decision and pressed send. I couldn't undo it.

Panchali went berserk, scolding me in front of everyone on the screen, spouting things like "inappropriate," "insensitive," and "disgusting." I told her to stop ranting and raving and remove herself from the thread if it upset her. She called me and we communicated briefly. While the exact words escape my memory, I recognize that we often utter things we don't mean to those we care about. We don't always have the chance to offer a heartfelt apology and make amends.

Months later, I heard through the grapevine that she had moved back home to be with her mother, who was terminally ill. She packed up her dogs, rented a car, and left her apartment in colossal disarray. One day, I got a call from my colleague in the building. "Doesn't your friend live on the fifth floor?" I told him she was in Virginia. "It's really weird, Sonya," he replied. "We've had a fire up there, and it seems to have started in her apartment."

The fire was confined to Panchali's unit, and I have a hunch the super took a match to it rather than paying to clean up the mess. Panchali never came back to New York. She was diagnosed with stage IV ovarian cancer. Because of her history and trust issues, she didn't go to doctors— certainly not OB/GYNs, even if they were female. She died on May 25th, 2016. Friends took her dogs in. We were devastated. She was a force in my world. I loved her to the moon and back and beyond. I am sorry that we fought and that I never said goodbye, or told her how much she meant to me. So many Thanksgivings, Christmases, and Easters blur together because she was always there, calling the table to order with a Hindu prayer. The walls would vibrate, and joy would bounce all over the room. Later that season, she was honored at the Tony Awards. I pictured her watching from a cloud or riding on a sunbeam draped in velvet, positively divaesque.

I've known many people with hoarding problems, both women and men. They all want the help even if they say they don't. They know they need it. Will they talk about who or what got them to that place? Sometimes yes, sometimes no. But you can read it in their stuff. You get the impression that they're protecting themselves with it, fortifying a wall to keep the evil spirits away. Every mess tells a different story, but it always feels the same. The stories must be shared. I hope Panchali knows I'm writing this for her. When I think of her, even now, looking over this chapter, reading this draft of the book, and crying, it feels like a loss—a huge, unfulfillable loss.

CHAPTER 3

Point by Point

One of my favorite children's stories is about a giant turtle: *The Legend of Mackinac Island.* It touches my heart, mostly because I love underdog tales. It's about what it means to be brave, trust in yourself, and endure.

Coincidentally, endurance is the game's name when traveling through Nepal and India. Traveling in a foreign country on that scale sparks the desire to converse with anyone and everyone, regardless of language or culture. It's the gift of just being with them, human to human. It was maddening and humbling—an incomparable experience.

Change is challenging; transitions are scary. Healing can be dangerous, too. It's all about trust: in the universe, in yourself—all that stuff they tell you in yoga class as we nod and say, "Yeah, I'm ready for it." But few are.

We all have to develop that hard outer shell. The goal is to keep softening the core underneath. You'll know when it's time to come out from the darkness when you're safe. The inside may not be as secure as you thought it was. That's the art of letting go. If it's meant to be, it'll always come back in one way or another.

Nepal attracts the best kind of visitors: big-hearted, spirited people. It took me a few weeks, but I learned to ease in and go with the flow. From there, my friend Terri and I ventured toward the Indian border to Ratnanagar and the Chitwan National Park. We saw Bengal tigers and a baby rhinoceros. We were riding on a local's truck up the mountainside when we first noticed that another Caucasian girl was hiking the area. She was a cute little pixie. Terri and I were sitting one day reading and journaling when she walked up to us and introduced herself as Julie from California. Two became three, and we've remained friends for almost twenty-five years.

On December 23, we crossed over to India and took a fifteen-hour bus ride to Varanasi in Uttar Pradesh. We spent Christmas Day walking the banks of the Ganges, watching bodies being cremated in the ceremonial "burning ghats."

It was unforgettable, the ultimate visual image of loss—and letting go. In America, we wear black, cry, go to a funeral home and then a church, write condolence cards, maybe talk about it, and say, OK, now deal with all the emotions. I was so naïve I didn't equate cremation with being burned. I never pictured the fire or the flames. It's as if you've been handed a bag of flour, and they tell you, this is flour, don't ask any questions about it; you don't need to know where it comes from or how it is made. In India, it's the opposite. You're smack dab in the middle of the wheat field with a gigantic, panoramic view of that flour from seedling to powder: birth, life, death, the whole shebang.

We stayed out of the big cities as much as possible. The locals were always curious about us, especially the boys, and people would come up to us and pat us down, feel our hair, and pinch our cheeks. No other culture is more "people-friendly." The three of us caused chatter everywhere we went. I remember standing at the train station of a tiny little town at 5:00 am, drinking chai out of saucers (the cups were all broken). Two bare-foot, bare-chested boys came to greet us. They signaled to their buddies, and within minutes, thirty men stood around us, asking, "What's your name? Where are you from? *Are you a movie star?*" I don't think they'd ever seen an American up close, let alone three twenty-some-thing American girls.

Food was another matter. We ate fresh yogurt every morning that we bought from the milk dealers. In the evening, they return to sell hot milk that they boiled. They'd hand it to us in little terracotta cups that you'd throw to the ground when you had finished. I'll never forget the cows walking by, breaking up hundreds of them with their hooves. I loved how they moved through the corridors of the small towns. I loved watching the monkeys steal things from people and wild peacocks preening in the town square.

Life was different after that, even in a city as exciting as New York. Being overseas made me feel more active and alive. I was only concerned with my own needs. My senses were on overload, and all I had to do was indulge in it. I had to confront who I was and what I wanted and needed. The pack on my back felt like a shell. *Mackinac Island* took on a more elaborate meaning: What do you need to carry, and what can you let go of? I had to justify what I was carrying and why. I enjoyed that clarity.

The essentials always have multiple purposes, and the more you focus on them, the quieter you can become with your authentic self. If hoarding is extreme, what's its opposite? The monks and the priests in their tiny rooms? Are they present in their mental spaces and the tangible area around them? I talk about this often with my clients and ask myself the same difficult questions.

I delighted in the vagabond life for nearly a year. It was undeniably transformative and revitalizing, but I also missed my home. I forgot how much I loved my mom's cooking and freshly-laundered sheets. When I returned to New York in the fall of 1997, I continued to work part-time as an organizer and move manager. 1998 is hazy for me now; it's all gray. We all have years like that. The older we get, the more of those years we may have. I had gotten good at walking in the Himalayas; I wasn't so good at wandering inside my head, staring at the wall of my childhood bedroom. I knew what I wanted. What was I waiting for?

First, I had to deal with a severe kidney infection that knocked me off my feet and landed me in the hospital. It could have been caused by residual parasites from copper pots in Nepalese villages, but we'll never know for sure.

It was a time of enormous change for me. Sometimes the physical body goes through changes while emotions are being purged. In any case, it was painful. My body was short-circuited, and I couldn't pay attention to anything but my health. Mom was in Florida, and I was utterly alone. Some of life's most important lessons come when we're achingly alone.

One of those lessons was not in Nepal or Turkey but in an emergency room in New York City. I watched a cleaning lady at the hospital use the same rag and bucket of water on every bed, counter, and floor. I thought, "OK, that's gross." I got my bare ass off the metal table I was sitting on, found some rubbing alcohol, and called a former client named Denise. Her husband was a doctor and professor at Mount Sinai Icahn School of Medicine. I called him and told him I needed help.

As luck would have it, he knew the Chief Medical Officer of my emergency room. Within fifteen minutes, I had my own room. It was then that I realized the life-altering power of networking. The wheels in my head were turning, and the gears were cranking so loudly that I couldn't wait to get out of that bed and start my business.

It was a pivotal moment for me. I wanted to take everything I had learned from every boss that had punctured or wounded me and do something different and better than what I had experienced. I started going to networking groups in the city. I know there are networking groups all over the country and the world, but there's nothing quite like doing it in New York.

Anyone who's gone through that gauntlet knows what I'm talking about. There's nothing more exciting than grabbing that bagel and coffee and shaking hands with the real Manhattan moneymakers.

My first group was a LeTip. Before my first meeting, I took the subway to Kate's Paperie. I had them create the most heavenly Celadon green textured business cards with purple ink. They didn't read "organizer" or anything except my name and a 212 phone number that I had piped into my room at the Majestic.

I could see my business like you'd see the picture of a puzzle on the back of the box. You have to spill all those itsy-bitsy pieces out on the table, spread them around, touch each one and fail many times before you can decode the pattern (remember, I'm good at puzzles!). I met all sorts of people at LeTip and started hiring people who could help me construct my business from soup to nuts. One was a graphic artist; the other was an all-purpose wordsmith, vocabulary whiz, and first-class researcher. I still needed to get employees and wanted to start hiring when I figured out the nitty-gritty.

The best place to begin was at the beginning, as they say. I asked all the stupid questions so I would remember everything. I called a business attorney and asked about the paperwork I needed to complete. We filed as an S corporation and registered the EIN and the NAICS codes. I spent hours on the phone with the Department of Labor, following up on things I had mailed or faxed to them.

Branding was also imperative. I knew my business couldn't be "Sonya's Closet" or some nonsense. I wanted a distinguished, one-word name that would age well. Something that I could put on a business card and hand to any attorney or financial planner in Midtown or Greenwich, or Miami Beach. I also wanted to create an environment for a team to expand and bring their talents and ideas to the room. Those ideas start with simple things like the logo, the colors, and the font—no detail should be considered insignificant. Seriatim is Latin for "in a series; taking one subject after another in regular order; one after another; point by point." As a Roman Catholic, I'd grown up simultaneously fearing and revering Latin. It was elegant without being imperious.

Then came my colors: blue and green. I've always been drawn to trees, especially trees next to the water, on a lake, or by a river. Trees equal expansion; water is calming. I had grown up by the water in San Francisco, where there were also redwood trees; we live on the island of Manhattan, surrounded by water; Cleveland is on the southern shore of Lake Erie; my father had unbelievably gorgeous blue eyes; I don't have the greenest thumb in the world, but I love being among plants, leaves, fruit, anything that represents our Mother Earth. Our work at Seriatim is about transformation: from a seedling to a tree. I always try to manifest an entire orchard for my clients, team, and myself—a boundless bounty.

In January of 1999, I rented an apartment with the man who's now my husband, Pete, on John Street in the

Financial District. That's still one of my favorite apartments. Around the same time, I got an office space on Walker and Broadway, built out desks, little tables, and filing cabinets, and had a fantastic little space there. I started reading every business book I could find and became completely absorbed in Michael Gerber's *The E-Myth Revisited.* I took a two-year correspondence course with his Radical U. I realized I was lousy with words. I had to hire an assistant who could write and be Seriatim's mouthpiece.

That's when I hired my first employee: Heather M. She had been a personal assistant at the Dakota, across the street from the Majestic. She studied playwriting at Columbia and was trying to make it in the theatre scene. She is incredibly gifted and still a dear friend. Thank goodness she had no organizing talent and was perfectly content being hunched over a computer putting ideas and words to ink and sending them out in the mail. Heather helped me create a Standard Operating Procedure that became the framework of the House of Seriatim.

A friend from her graduate program, Alex L. (still a friend and a rock), came aboard to craft brochures, stationery, envelopes, cards—everything but the kitchen sink. In 1999, the relocation industry was still paper-based. He also helped me up with my first manual with a training process for future hires. He and Heather's *chef-d'oeuvre* was a "screenplay" for a promotional video that I still have on a DVD. (I've kept everything related to my business's history.)

Sonya Weisshappel

Meanwhile, I was also getting to know the top local movers in the city. I wanted something other than a national company. I wanted people based in the five boroughs, New Jersey or Connecticut, who knew the ins and outs of the co-op politics and city traffic. Heather called everyone in the phone book and set up appointments for them to come to the Upper West Side. I met Vincent— Vinny—through networking. He was from Ireland, young, quick-witted, and willing to do things my way.

Our first job together was with Ms. M in Harlem. She was one of my favorites, a senior, and a total spitfire of a character. Originally from Texas, Ms. M lived on Adam Clayton Powell, Jr. Boulevard and 112th Street. Because the real estate was showing an upward trend (read: gentrification), Ms. M wanted to make sure she and her fellow senior citizens in the building were protected. She successfully fought with the city to purchase the building from HUD for one dollar. She was a hell of a negotiator.

There was a catch, though. They all had to move into temporary housing to seal the deal while the city got the five-story, ten-unit brownstone up to code. She called me and said, "We're a bunch of old people, and we've lived in this building together for decades. We haven't moved in years. Can you help?" How could I say no?

I remember standing in Ms. M's kitchen, having a glass of water with Vinny, standing side by side. Every door in the house was open, and the residents and their family members were wailing in the stairwell. He sighed and said, "This is awful; I can't believe you do this for a living. I can't believe you help people do this." I couldn't agree or disagree. All I could think was: If not me, then who? Some tenants couldn't afford the mover, so I pitched in.

I had to teach them which box to use for the heavier stuff and how to pack and tape it up—Moving 101. Reliving it now, it was complete mayhem. These seniors' homes and lives had gone topsy-turvy. I was thinking the job was going to be an utter failure. By whatever miracle, we got them into temporary housing, unpacked them, and waited to move them back in so we could empty them again. Ms. M became one of the Grande Dames of the neighborhood. She also became the landlord of her building and helped several of my employees sublet apartments. That building and its residents were part of Seriatim's history for decades.

I had hardly begun to find my footing when life in New York was about to be altered dramatically. I was working in New Jersey on September 10, 2001. By a fluke, I also had an employee doing a play there (I hired many actors and writers). He'd pick me up at the PATH train in his car and drop me at the job site on the way to rehearsal. I said, "If your rehearsal goes late tonight, leave me a voicemail, and I'll meet you at 10:00 instead of 9:00." I didn't have anything crucial. It was mainly getting a house ready for a big party; the client was returning from the Poconos on the fourteenth.

On the morning of the eleventh, I was dressed and having a cup of tea. I dialed my voicemail (remember doing that?) and got my employee's message confirming 10 o'clock. I hung up the phone and sipped my tea. The weather was splendid, with only sunlight and a clear, blue sky. We had incredible windows that faced northward toward City Hall. At that instant, I heard a noise. Loud. What could it be? A ten-ton truck thumping over metal plates? It's New York; ignore it. Pete awoke and asked me what it was. I shrugged. "No clue." He put his head back on the pillow. "Severe, though, wasn't it?"

Suddenly, papers go flying by—reams and reams accumulating on the street and blanketing the windshields of parked cars. "Is it a ticker-tape parade?" Pete replied, "It's only 9 o'clock; why would there be a parade?" All at once, I saw hefty chunks of spongy, yellow fiberglass insulation outside, blowing in the wind. It was like a cotton candy machine went haywire, hurling fuzzy, prickly debris everywhere.

Pete stood up. The phone began to ring. My girlfriend Sharon had just been married the weekend before and was in Australia on her honeymoon. She said she was eating dinner and watching the news. One of the Towers had been hit by a plane. "Get out!" she cried, "Get out!" I told Pete to get dressed and called my mom's phone. I knew her routine and that she'd be at the gym, but I had to leave her a message to let her know we were all right. There was a lot of commotion outside. At this point, the TV was on. We saw the other plane hit. This was no accident.

I'll always remember the hours that followed. As the first tower fell, the sky turned pitch-black. The apartment began to rumble like we were having an earthquake. It was so extreme that we gripped each other; I thought the floor would cave in. We weren't sure if we should use the power, so we lit candles. I looked out the window. I felt like I was underwater; I could perceive things floating by in the dark. Time slowed. Claustrophobia set in. We heard pigeons lining up on the windowsill; they had gathered on every inch of the ledge, pushing their faces onto the glass.

I snapped pictures of the apartment, fed the goldfish, grabbed a couple of pairs of underwear, and wetted two bandanas to put around our faces. We walked down the stairs and out the door and headed north towards the Upper West Side. The rubbish was up to our shins, all burnt like sand. We talked to nearly every person we met along the way, hugging them, asking if they were OK, tears streaming down our faces. We stayed at Mom's that night, watching the news for hours in disbelief. The whole world did the same.

We came back to John Street and stayed downtown until January 2005. The area may have seemed like a war zone, but I never felt unsafe. Our landlord raised the rent, so we moved to 25 Broad Street. The weekends were still quiet, and we'd stroll for hours and look at architecture or sit on the benches by the water and read. Hundreds of workers began digging out the site where the towers had been, and we had a bird's eye view from our rooftop. We invited all our friends over to glimpse the reconstruction and rejuvenation. It was American history happening in front of our eyes.

9/11 made me want to stay in New York. I never had that level of fear. We loved our life downtown and stayed there as long as it made sense for our family. My little office on Walker Street was the best; I had all the tables made and bought lots of new equipment. As an organizer, I think a lot about the future and how to plan for unanticipated events. I like to play offense as much as possible. I kept seeing those papers drifting by the window.

I knew I had to create redundancies for my data and the client's personal and professional files. I got a server the size of a mini-fridge and also started backing things up on the cloud, first through Amazon S3 and later on Intuit Quickbase. The contentment lasted only a short time. One morning, I discovered a note on my desk: "Building being sold, six weeks to vacate." What was I going to do?

Pete and I decided to get married. I got pregnant two and a half months later. After Beverly was born, I went back to work almost straight away. We moved to an apartment on Front Street that didn't have an elevator. Even the snobbiest New Yorkers would cringe at the thought of carrying the stroller up three flights of stairs! Mom was coming down, and I was going up all the time. Commuting via public transportation is hard enough; a baby makes it doubly challenging. I'd wrap little Bev up in the Bjorn and go. Sometimes I'd forget the pump or the bottle or bring ten diapers instead of twelve or two outfits instead of three. And if I'm organized, how do other people do it? We endured it for as long as we could. Seven-hundred square feet weren't going to cut it anymore. The new year was a new beginning. That January, we put our things in storage and moved in with Mom. It was a step back that ended up moving my family forward.

I loved our home on Central Park West. Everyone had their little corner. Mom stayed in her room where she could smoke cigarettes and watch TV peacefully. Bev took my old room. Pete and I set up our bedroom in the library. Against my better judgment, we installed an extra TV in the living room. Never in my life had there been a television set in that room. I don't particularly appreciate looking at screens in sitting rooms where people should eat, drink, and chat. We had few options, so I kept my snootiness in check. We spent many evenings in that room. Sometimes I'd work late, and Pete would have a drink and watch the news in that big, cozy chair. He quickly developed a penchant for falling asleep there.

Behind that big chair, my grandmother's black resin turtle sat on a little table. He was about as big around as the bottom of a coffee cup. His shell was completely removable, revealing space for jewelry or a trinket. It was a sentimental heirloom, not a valuable antique. My lifelong love of Testudines may have begun with this tiny treasure. I told Pete, "Don't you dare let that chair push against that table!" One fateful evening, Murphy's law proved legitimate. Somehow the table was nudged with sufficient force to send Mr. Turtle to the floor. He lost a leg amidst the chaos; we knew it would take more than Elmer's glue to repair the damage.

I commenced an internet search for people with special fix-it skills. Keep in mind: Google was less advanced than it is now. I didn't know what words to use, but I knew there was someone somewhere in the five boroughs of New York who could help. Growing up in San Francisco, Aunt Josephine ran to and from wood shops, glass cutters, and marble quarries. I knew I'd find the right person if I put my mind to it. I came across a webpage that was more like an electronic business card—we'd call it a landing page in today's terminology. Ark Restorations. I liked the name. The owners were Ukrainian, and the shop was located on West 37th Street, near Penn Station.

After a short ride on the C train, I was there. It was comfortable and inviting, with lots of books and objects. In every cranny, something creative. They told me they could fix him and gave me a yellow paper. "Come back in a few weeks," said the wife. I got home, handed the paper to Pete, and said, "Tag, you're it! Don't forget!"

Work, travel, kids, and life got in the way, as it always does. Weeks turned into months, and that yellow piece of paper must have been thrown into the garbage because we couldn't find it anywhere. What was the name of the shop? Park Restorations? No, it wasn't near the park. It was near Penn Station. As you must know by now, dear reader, I'm not good with words or names, but I can remember faces and places, and I knew if I could get to the right block, I'd remember the building and the lobby. I had no receipt, address, or turtle—but I knew it was east of Ninth Avenue, west of Sixth, north of Penn, and south of Times Square. So whenever I was in that area, I took a breath and did what every New Yorker does: walk around until you get where you want to be.

It took me a couple of months, but I finally found it. I knew it was on the south side of the street, near a dress shop, in the middle of the block. When I arrived, the building directory confirmed my hopes with three simple letters: A-R-K. I exited the elevator, walked down the hall-way—it was all so familiar!—and rang the bell. The door opened. The Ukrainian woman squinted at me and asked, "What took you so long?!" We had a good laugh, and she invited me in. "I love turtles," she said. "I am a turtle. That is my animal!" "Mine too," I replied. "Mine too!"

I learned that her name was Rena. "We have things on our shelves for years," she told me. "People die, and they leave them here. Let me go find your turtle." While she went rummaging for it, her husband, Toly, took over as host and entertainer. He felt like someone I'd known in a past life. From there, the friendship took an accel-erated path. It has been a gift. Both Rena and Toly are incredible gifts. They met as teenagers and fled Ukraine together before the collapse of the Soviet Union. They're real Renaissance people, compulsively creative, enviably balanced in a yin-yang way.

I later learned that they were go-to repair gurus for Sotheby's and Christie's and many individual collectors and museums. If something falls and gets chipped, they're the people to call. They're also the best at telling fakes. They know what was made when and where, the materials, and the art-making process. They can tell you the earliest version of something, who mastered it, who copied it, and why it is or isn't worth something today. They've never been interested in fads or trends; they know and care about artistry and craftsmanship.

Over time, their little shop—"Narnia"—became important in my life. If I were in the neighborhood, I'd stop in to use the bathroom and have a cup of tea. When I am there, I don't feel like I'm in New York or anywhere else; I feel like I've disappeared. It's marvelous. Bev was at a friend's one Friday evening, and Pete and I went over for a drink. It was a historic night, the four of us drinking vodka together for the first time. Now, I love a good vodka cranberry, but I don't have the highest tolerance in the world, and I can't drink as much as Toly! Rena doesn't drink much, either, but we all felt like we needed a break from the world for whatever reason.

We were having a grand time when—presto—we'd suddenly polished off a bottle and a half of Balinoff. Pete thought he was OK until he tried to get up from his chair. The joke was on us.

All I remember is that Toly had to drive us home, and we spent three days in bed detoxing. It was one of my favorite nights in New York, not because anything particularly special or magical happened, but because I felt a sense of rightness and belonging that I "fit." Somehow, despite New York's unruliness and changeability, I'd found the people that I wanted to be an adult with. It was a subtle yet remarkable feeling.

Whenever Seriatim does a job somewhere outside of the city, I'm amazed by how easy it all seems to be. How practical. You ask people to show up at a specific time, and they do. You don't have to beg, bribe, or steer around dozens of hurdles. You're like, wow, my day's over at 3 pm, how lovely—what should I do? But that doesn't make me feel calm. It doesn't make me want to grab a book and a cup of hot tea and sit on the couch. It makes me nervous. I recently realized that I needed New York, missed it when I was away and wanted to be among its spunky, occasionally aggressive full-timers. I need an elbowing on the subway now and then. I want to be around artists and creative thinkers, and overachievers. Other places, even California, can sometimes shut down and seem close-minded. Not New York City. There's an openness and tolerance politically, religiously, and socially that you can't find anywhere else. Don't even bother looking for it elsewhere.

My husband, stepsons, and daughter were all born there; it's their home base. My mom loves Manhattan and will probably never leave it. She is one of my best friends, and that won't change. I built my business here in New York, and I'm grateful for that every single day. I get up and say a happy little prayer. But ever since 9/11, I know where the nearest exit is.

CHAPTER 4

Slowly but Steadily

O h, the power of networking! I was at a LeTip meeting when a real estate attorney told me he had a client who needed relocation assistance. "He comes from a family of Manhattan garmentos and has a large duplex in SoHo with a private rooftop," he said. "He has a few animals, too." The job was a game-changer for me and Seriatim, but "few" was a formidable understatement.

The building on Hudson Street was unassuming; the lobby was equally modest. I took the elevator up and rang the doorbell. Mr. R appeared at the door. Before entering, I could hear strange sounds: crickets chirping, water percolating, incidental splashes, and mechanical murmuring. The air felt balmy, misty, and semi-tropical, with a strong whiff of cedar. Not horrible, but not savory. Four large filtration systems created constant bubbling noises. The unit was at least 25,000 square feet and seemed to me like a football field, only with lots of tiny enclosures.

Within those designated areas were hundreds of live animals, primarily small- and medium-sized tortoises, turtles, and terrapins, in or around kiddie pools. There were a few massive ones as well. Snakes and lizards, too—even rabbits! Their food? Dead rats, fresh vegetables, and hundreds, if not thousands, of worms and crickets, had to be delivered daily and stored in one of the dozen refrigerators on the premises. It was larger than any pet store in the city. It was an actual mixed-species habitat with its ecosystem.

Mr. R's two floors ran the entire building's length, undergoing extensive repairs. Somehow, the workers had broken through the roof's thermoplastic membrane, and rainwater had flooded. The ceilings were over eighteen feet high, and it was difficult to patch up the damage. The leaks were getting worse by the day. Many of the animals were from the Brazilian rainforest, which doesn't have the same types of bacteria we do. If water touched the wrong place or started flowing in a different direction too quickly, it could have killed certain species. Mr. R was entangled in a series of legal battles with the roofers, the contractor, and even other shareholders in the building. No one wanted to accept responsibility for the damaged roof, and Mr. R was getting desperate. He hired me instantly. It was a combination of good timing and a certain lucky charm my husband, Pete, gave me: a turtle ring.

In the years leading up to Y2K, SoHo was the booming hotbed of the dot-com bubble. The live-work-play model was in vogue, and real estate moguls were gobbling up parts of downtown's west side for newly-made millionaire twenty-somethings to gut and refashion any way they pleased. Beer was the new coffee, and table tennis matches replaced business meetings. Mr. R's property was a perfect fit for this new vision of twenty-first-century office space, and he could find a buyer quickly. Finding the right place—or places—to house his menagerie was quite a different matter. The job took nearly six months to complete.

Mr. R told me it all started when he was offered turtle soup at a Chinatown restaurant. He decided to buy the turtle and take it home instead. Many people keep reptiles as pets but don't possess Mr. R's compulsive propensity. He only took a few years to become a renowned amateur herpetologist. The Port Authority police started calling him about animals impounded or confiscated. He'd go to JFK airport at all hours to retrieve them and stay up all night, setting up their abodes. Most of the time, he ended up housing them permanently. He wasn't merely a collector. He was a caregiver.

In addition to his animal collection, Mr. R kept his family's archives, a mini-Library of Congress. They housed essential documents from the early days of the midtown garment industry and fabric samples from all over the world. Some were woven with real gold and silver. This portion of his move required an inventory the size of a standard client's project. We also had to research how to transport and store these antique textiles so they would be protected.

Confessions of a Chaos Whisperer

I talked to Heather, and we both agreed that it was time to hire more field crew. I was lucky to find Nicole, who worked with Seriatim for many years. She was at Mr. R's daily while I searched for apartments with him. We also found help from certain animal rescue groups that sent volunteers to feed and maintain the animals. Each animal or group of animals had special needs. There were refrigerators for crickets and others for dead rats. How many pounds of fresh vegetables need to be delivered per day? What's the feeding schedule? Who can be moved in the morning, and who has to wait until the late afternoon? Which ones need to remain in the space until the last possible minute? Will the elevators at the new building be wide enough and strong enough to accommodate the filtration systems? What can be consolidated? What do we need? Nicole and I called conservation experts at the Bronx Zoo. They were enormously helpful in helping to plan the actual relocation.

Mr. R spent tremendous money and effort on his animals, and their care occupied nearly every waking moment of his life for fifteen years. The move was an important lesson for him. The collection had grown past the point of control. No one person could be expected to keep going, even with the help of volunteers. I admired Mr. R, but he was a complex, demanding person. There was no way of ever knowing what he was thinking; I couldn't read him like my other clients. Despite his compulsive and occasionally outlandish behavior, he possessed true genius.

Initially, we planned to redistribute the two floors between two separate apartments on Canal Street. It still wasn't enough. We ended up renting a third. He wanted to remain close to JFK airport so he could continue his efforts to rescue animals that had been abandoned or illegally trafficked. We began prepping the move once I knew where his bed and personal items would be. We separated the nocturnal or sick animals, who had to be near Mr. R during the night. Before Mr. R signed the leases, I suggested we bring in a structural engineer to ensure the apartments were sturdy enough for the equipment. Certain tanks had to be stacked on each other rather than placed side by side. One of the tanks barely cleared the ceiling of the new apartment. Those installations required professional plumbers who specialized in aquarium filters.

The move cost a fortune. We opted for a piecemeal approach, and movers showed up in small groups over ten days. The process, like his turtles, moved slowly out of necessity. The animals had to be protected during transit. It was a total production with many moving parts—and, in some cases, legs hopping and jumping. We also used the Man with a Van a lot, and many Tupperware containers needed to be sanitized before and after use. We also had to keep our own hands clean as much as possible.

In the middle of the biggest job of my life, I booked another. It was a neighbor and friend of Mr. R's. They couldn't have been more different. She was a mom of three kids with no pets. Her husband was an advertising executive who had to stop working after a freak scuba diving accident. I never got the whole story, but his gear must have malfunctioned, and he was underwater too long. He had permanent brain damage that affected whatever cortex was responsible for empathy and compassion. It was like *Regarding Henry* in reverse. They ended up getting a divorce, but only after I moved them to a new apartment.

The newly-formed Seriatim team helped Mr. R settle into his new apartment. He'd spend his days running back and forth, feeding and caring for his beloved animals. Sooner or later, though, he burned himself out. He kept saying yes until he could not give or do more. He cherished each one of the amphibians or reptiles as anyone would their dog or cat, but they had become an obsession, a curse. He was a loner, never truly comfortable with having help. I also think he enjoyed having control and feeling like he had a purpose. He is also whip-smart and sensible enough to let go when the time is right. He found a place in New Jersey. The kind folks at the Bronx Zoo also recommended a nearby sanctuary that could host many animals.

I'd call Mr. R on his birthday or send him holiday cards in the following years. I like keeping in touch with my clients. I think about my dear Mr. Turtle almost every day. He did so much good for so many living things. Working on his project was my way of caring for the caregiver. It was my ideal, *Catcher-in-the-Rye* job. He taught me how to take my love of animals further and investigate ways to support rescue here in the city. He also taught me what it meant to care. I had to create a logistical plan for his family's archives, vendors, personal items, and the improbable three-ring circus that was his métier and his passion.

So much depended on me. It was an extraordinary feeling, and I longed for another job that could challenge me in such a way. But there can only be one inimitable Mr. R.

CHAPTER 5

The Owl Collector

I don't remember a final conversation with my dad or even his last words, but I remember hearing his voice years after he died. I went into our old den, facing 72nd Street, got out a tape, put it in my Walkman, and hit play. There he was. He was talking to me. My dad was talking to me. I burst into tears; hearing him speak again was so unexpected and beautiful. What a blessing, those possessions that enable us to reconnect with our past.

When our past becomes a source of psychological harm, and we find ourselves engulfed by these objects on a daily basis, decluttering transforms from a life-changing endeavor to a potentially life-saving act.

Mr. V was a "Newport Casual" kind of guy: gold-buttoned blue blazer, topsiders, and khakis. He was soft-spoken, almost whispery, and oh-so-kind. "Contemplative" is a good adjective for him—also "naughty," but in a good way. His looks weren't overly quaffed or polished, but his taste was exacting, opinionated, and refined.

His spacious four-bedroom apartment was full of precious objects, including his collection of owls. There were hundreds in all different shapes and sizes. I was amazed by how much he knew about fine china—there were probably thirty or more eighteen-piece dinnerware sets. The apartment must have been magnificent in its heyday, but that didn't matter much. Mr. V had lost everything of fundamental importance in life.

His daughter died tragically in a hang glider accident in Glen Cove, on the north shore of Long Island, and his wife never recovered. She later died of a broken heart. Every time he walked through the door, he was greeted by memories of his wife and daughter. Remnants of knitting projects were scattered about, bags and bags of yarn and a large Aubusson needlepoint carpet, sadly unfinished.

I helped him downsize to a rental apartment on East 72nd Street. He was willing to reduce but wasn't ready to let it all go. He still kept hundreds of books and DVDs. My team and I arranged to have shelves built and painted. It gave new life to some of his wonderful objects, including the owls. He couldn't part with his art collection. Crozier came and hung dozens of his paintings on the Kermit-green walls, crowded together impressively.

He called me now and then, and we would talk about our lives, how we felt about things. Sometimes we'd speak for an hour or more. Now that I look back on it, I was the same age his daughter would have been. That didn't occur then, but it must have informed me so much about our friendship.

I soon realized that Mr. V had financial problems. The bank had repossessed his home in Glen Cove. He had walked away from it and never looked back, abandoning all his belongings and the horrible memories. Then his attorney entered the picture. This man—I'll call him Mr. A—was supposed to be a trusted advisor, monitoring the purse strings. Mr. V didn't have a better way of watching it. We didn't yet have smartphones and tablets. He didn't have a computer. I saw him use a flip phone once or twice.

Mr. V was very lonely. He had an odd loyalty to Mr. A, or maybe it was indebtedness. Whether it was out of guilt, fear, or previous wrongdoings, I'll never know for sure. Mr. V lived a very lavish lifestyle and had significant expenses. They both knew he was living beyond his means. Mr. A was ruthless, scheming, and entitled. He began to pressure Mr. V to sell the apartment and liquidate whatever items he could. He called a prominent auction house on the Upper East Side. Mr. A told me to have the most expensive articles wrapped, packed, and delivered on time—"Don't ask any questions, and don't talk to Mr. V," he told me. That's when I realized the auction house would give him a kickback. I had to intervene.

I'll always remember the call from Mr. V. "Sonya, I need your help. I need you to come over as soon as you can." So I did. "Mr. A was here," he said, wringing his hands. "And he is going to have someone hand me a check for fifteen thousand dollars." I asked what they were planning to take. "Everything," he replied. "I think I'm in trouble. I need the cash. But this can't be right."

The auction house in Manhattan had offered to pay him a fixed price rather than a percentage of the sale. It happens all the time. For some people, having the money upfront can be a blessing, especially for purchasing or renting a new apartment. But I knew Mr. V's instincts were right. I had seen nice things before that had fetched heavy sums at auction, and I knew Mr. V's stuff was of the same high quality. I picked up the phone and called my friend John, an auctioneer in New Jersey. "Can you come today?" I asked. John quickly looked around the apartment and immediately offered to match the fifteen thousand as a down payment plus the auction proceeds.

The movers made the delivery to New Jersey the same week. That fall, the contents sold for over ninety thousand dollars. Mr. V got over seventy-five thousand dollars after the auctioneer's cut and the mover fees.

I could hear Mr. A practically jumping up and down on the other end of the phone, screaming at the top of his lungs. Oh, he was furious! He had given clear instructions for me to butt out, and, of course, I had done the opposite. I told him I had nothing to be ashamed of; I was only doing what was best for Mr. V. Then he said something interesting: "How dare you take away the pieces I was promised?"

One piece, in particular: a little inlay table that probably had some historical value. It ended up on the cover of the auction house's brochure. I told him he should have called and placed a bid if he wanted it badly. He hung up, and I never heard from him again. He knew he had done the wrong thing and could have been disbarred. It could have been much worse. I am grateful for how it turned out. I've carried the lesson with me ever since and have repeated the story to hundreds of clients.

Mr. V soon found another rental on East 72nd Street, and my team helped him move in. It was a terrific location, and the apartment had a beautiful view. I had a handyman build new shelves for his books and owl collection. (It's so hard to find good handymen.) Mr. V's style, however, had been reduced to the utilitarian: a bed, a sofa, a few end tables—not much else. It didn't matter; he was happy. We all were. I occasionally kept in touch with Mr. V to ensure he was all right. I knew his health was declining.

A few years later, I got a call from Mr. V's nephew in California. I had never heard of him; I didn't know Mr. V had any family left. They thought it was time for Mr. V to move into a nursing home, and I agreed. His nephew had found the perfect one near his home in La Jolla. But there was a catch: How would they get him there? As their luck would have it, I was already set to go to Los Angeles to attend my cousin Jennifer's wedding. My husband, mother, and three-year-old daughter were coming, too. We bought Mr. V a ticket and made the arrangements. I packed what was left of his apartment into a small moving truck. The nephew sent me the address of the assisted living facility, and the movers did the rest.

There was one thing left undone, something I had to complete before Mr. V left New York: his wife's needlepoint carpet. I found a lovely Turkish woman who was an expert embroiderer by chance. The result was stunning: vivid, Easter-egg green circles, pink rose with brown stems, utterly royal. It had found its purpose again. I had honored Mr. V's past without dwelling on sadness or loss. In a way, that carpet became more valuable than anything Mr. V had sent to auction. It was part of his personal history.

It was a long plane ride. Mother, husband, baby, client. That's the image that sticks with me. We met Mr. V's nephew at the airport and shook hands. I hugged my friend, and we parted ways. That was the last time I saw him. About two years later, I unpacked Christmas ornaments and found a little owl. It was like Mr. V saying hi to me. I called his nephew and left a voicemail, saying I was thinking of them and wishing them happy holidays. He called me back the next day. "You thought of him just as he was passing. That was his way of saying goodbye." I believe that's true.

I can always tell when people are lonely, and I've always had a soft spot for older people. It's also part of life in New York, seeing them in the buildings where we live and work, in the lobbies, streets, and parks. People in other places chose to spread out, suburbanize, tint their car windows, and actively ignore what's often in plain sight: the good and the bad. While creating space for ourselves is essential, we should never sacrifice the ability to see and hear others.

Owls may look or sound scary, but they're bluffing. They'd never hurt you and are pretty tender on the inside. That was Mr. V to a T.

CHAPTER 6

The Secret Stash

Wills and estate plans often present intricate provisions, clauses, and ideas that pose significant challenges in their execution. As a professional organizer operating nationwide, I encounter the diverse regulations of each state, including the recurring demand for equitable distribution in New York. While intentions may be good, equity is a difficult objective to attain.

When an individual desires a specific item that falls under the "equitable distribution" umbrella that wasn't explicitly bequeathed to them, questions of fairness arise among siblings. Can compensation bridge the gap, and how do we navigate the ever-changing value of these objects? Appraisal and selling prices diverge, complicating matters further. This conundrum ignited a heated dispute between the Brothers G, two adult siblings with a fractured relationship.

Hurdles arise when a will mandates equitable distribution of household contents among family members.

Valuation discrepancies emerge, pitting a $100 piece of furniture against its $5,000 counterpart, with each sibling holding individual preferences. Achieving real equity becomes an elaborate puzzle. Must every possession be reduced to a monetary sum? Furthermore, how do these considerations impact negotiations if the estate fails to cover relocation costs?

Parents should ask questions like: What holds significance? What fits your space? What can be easily passed on to others? Such considerations hold transformative potential. Attorneys must guide clients toward comprehensive estate planning that embraces the intricacies of our desires and legacies.

But what happens if specific items that are mentioned in a will cannot be located? Have they gone missing? Have they been stolen? Or do they still reside within the home, requiring a thorough search through suitcases, pockets, and drawers in the hope of rediscovery?

This scenario was one of the most confounding aspects of Mr. O's estate. It is precisely at this juncture that the organizer's expertise becomes indispensable. Mr. O's body had been found in his Manhattan townhouse. He had no heat or hot water and had frozen to death. Pete and I saw it in the newspaper one morning and were stunned. How could it be?

He lived in a multimillion-dollar piece of real estate on the East Side but died of hypothermia like a homeless person, totally undignified. The gas had been cut off following a lengthy dispute with ConEdison. How does a person end up like that? Had he turned his back on his friends and family, or had he been discarded? I cannot even imagine the desperation, the isolation, the crippling loneliness. But I felt it when I entered that space again.

When I showed up to bid on the estate clearing in the summer of 2018, it wasn't the first time I had been in Mr. O's house. I'd been inside at least nine years before that occasion. My mother, Joyce, a Corcoran broker, met him on the street outside his building. He asked her to take a look and tell him what he could get for it. She told him it was impossible to sell it in its condition, so she told him about me and my business and gave him my phone number.

When I told Pete I'd be going to Murray Hill to visit him and give a quote, he stopped and turned pale. "You won't do anything of the kind. Don't you know who he is?" I honestly didn't. At one time, Mr. O had run with New York's most elite crowd of socialites and spectacular stars. He had gone to boarding school in Switzerland and had been everywhere and had friends on nearly every continent.

"I was in high school," Pete recalled. "He was always after young girls—underage girls—and would offer them drugs. Expensive drugs. The kind you give to debutantes. He asked me if I'd come to his house and bring my girlfriend. I didn't know any better; I thought he would give us free alcohol, which he did. We knocked on the door and heard a voice call out, 'Come on in!' He told us to fix ourselves a drink and make ourselves comfortable from the top of the staircase. He came down in his bathrobe and nothing else. At one point, he took out his rifle, stuck it out the window, and fired it at a stop sign! I can't believe the man never got arrested."

Nevertheless, I was more than a bit curious about the job. Perhaps I wanted to see the specter for myself. Even then, the house was a crumbling, chaotic mess. The exterior had a sad, lonely look. Mr. O had that, too. Like any eccentric New Yorker on the street or subway, he had the air of a mad scientist. His was hair like Christopher Lloyd's in *Back to the Future*, and he had a frantic manner of speaking, like something on an audio track had been sped up. He was what we used to call a "shut-in," but a high-functioning one. He could go out for a paper and a coffee but couldn't take more than a few steps outside an established diameter from Second Avenue to Park. We'll never know if that was by choice.

I assume he had obsessive-compulsive disorder. He told me his private wealth manager monitored his expenses and kept him in a basic routine with his finances. Now that I think about it, it was probably a cry for help.

Based on his clutter, I believe he was a victim of abuse. Had he ever gotten treatment? Had his illness been diagnosed but then ignored? Something had been festering, and you could see, smell, and feel it. At first glance, you think it's a spooky, abandoned house. Then you realize a brand-new vacuum cleaner is in the corner (likely unused). There wasn't a single piece of art hanging on the walls, but several gilt-framed paintings sitting on the floor propped up against a chair or sideboard. Disorder reigned: wires dangling, paint peeling, plaster falling, banisters detached. There was clear evidence of rats or other vermin having been in nearly every room and clutter up to your thighs.

"I'm in the midst of a renovation," he told me, which was partially correct. The parlor room had stacks of two-by-fours, wood siding, and trim. Either he ran out of money, was too kooky for the contractor, or abandoned the job because of the lack of electricity. Most likely, all of the above. There was an enormous kitchen that he loved being in because it had light. It was the kind of kitchen everyone wanted in New York City. The house had good light, in general. But nothing felt clean and or well-kept. In one room on the garden level, I encountered the most humongous piece of mold I've ever seen. Water must have crept through the skylight and onto the ceiling—a cluster of giant, gelatinous mushrooms. Downstairs, in the basement, he had a relatively new washer and dryer set, but it hadn't even been connected. Again, he hadn't paid ConEd.

Years later, when a bank trust department hired the Seriatim team to declutter, organize, and inventory the contents of the house, it was an all-hands-on-deck job. Since there was no running water, we arranged to install a porta-potty in the upstairs bathroom. The bank required our bags to be checked by a private security officer every time we exited the premises, even if we were going across the street for lunch or a breath of fresh air.

The bank wanted the job done quickly. We arranged to have particular objects sold, donated, or sent to Mr. O's family members, who were the very definition of "estranged." It was like a treasure hunt. I already knew there were Rolex watches and was expecting to find other fine things, not to mention essential papers needed for the estate. Also, photos and memorabilia for his children— whether or not they wanted to keep them, that wasn't up to me or my team. It was our job to uncover them.

Stuff seemed to flow in tidal waves: old newspapers, magazines, and plastic bags mixed in with tools and office supplies. There were massive piles of unwashed clothing next to packets of unused, unopened T-shirts and under-wear—total randomness. But you couldn't merely scoop it all up and toss it. There were donatable and auction-worthy items: new white shirts still in their dry cleaning bags, Glenmuir cashmere tangled in soiled bedsheets, and a collection of thirty-some vintage Rolex watches, every single one of Sotheby's quality. He also had kitschy things in cabinets and drawers, silver spoons, and little decorative souvenirs. We also found out about his sportscars, all parked in various garages on the east side and midtown. Lord knows when he had driven them last, if he had ever driven them at all.

We determined that he had been sleeping in his bed-room on a twin mattress surrounded by dunes of clothing, with hundreds of shirts piled up layer upon layer (tags still attached). Likewise, the path from the hallway to the mattress was labyrinthine, as if he had been hiding. Masses of clutter had blocked the main door to the main bedroom. You could only enter the room through a bathroom in the hallway, then through another small closet space. I believe this is symptomatic of being hurt or abused in some way. He must have felt too vulnerable during sleep and constructed a barrier, the nest a mother mouse makes for her babies.

It's as if he was trying to bury himself alive. Quite literally—he died on his bed. His stuff took all the oxygen away. It accumulated like one big parasite, a constant drone of static electricity. I heard that noise when I walked inside the house. It was as if you'd turned on ten thousand computers and left them with their screensavers rotating all day and all night. That was the feeling I had looking at his space and objects, their nonsensical rhythms and hollow reverberations.

Having that seven-story townhouse may have been a way of protecting his ego. The outside world didn't have to know about his dirty, dark secrets. Some of it could have been entitlement. He had lived on the edge with fast cars and dangerous drugs. Was it a death wish? Or fear? Perhaps he was forever wounded, like Nabokov's Humbert Humbert, searching for his Annabel.

The Seriatim team finished the job by hook or crook in less than a month. When the movers took away countless debris trucks, we breathed differently. The house itself must have breathed again. There weren't the same loud noises inside my head. At last, there was a bit of quiet.

I was told someone purchased the property from the bank and planned to renovate it. Whenever I'm on the east side, on my way to a museum or a potential project, I'll stroll by that house and whisper a little prayer. A prayer that a young family will find it and bring it all their love. When that happens, it will be a joyful day.

CHAPTER 7

Finding True Value

In a world where material possessions often symbolize status and prosperity, the temptation to acquire valuable objects can be overwhelming. We invest our dreams, aspirations, and hard-earned resources into these treasures, hoping they will enrich our lives. But what if the real value or worth of an object doesn't align with its outward appearance?

To answer this question, I'll give you two of my favorite examples: Mrs. S and Mrs. L.—polar opposites in almost every way imaginable.

Mr. and Mrs. S lived a life of luxury in a brownstone in the West 60s near Central Park, their wealth and success evident in the grandeur of their surroundings and décor. The tale of their fateful Persian rug serves as a testament to comprehending the value of our belongings and the fragility of our perceptions about them.

Mrs. S loved to embark on shopping sprees. On one occasion, she was accompanied by her designer and felt peculiarly uninhibited. The binge culminated in acquiring a quarter-million-dollar Persian rug. The designer, ever the opportunist, gladly collected a commission. Amid her exhilaration, Mrs. S omitted a crucial step: getting an appraisal. Ignorant of its value, Mrs. S returned home with nothing more than a receipt, unknowingly setting a series of events into motion.

Mr. S dutifully submitted the receipt to their insurance agent, who added the rug to their policy with a replacement value of $250,000. They diligently paid the insurance premiums, safeguarding their prized possession against the perils of fire or flood. In the case of the S family, it wasn't a natural disaster but rather Mr. S's affair with their daughter's best friend that shattered the illusion of their idyllic existence.

As the divorce proceedings unfolded, decisions had to be made about the distribution of their assets. They agreed to sell their Upper West Side home, and the rug was consigned to storage. In a bittersweet exchange, Mrs. S paid Mr. S $125,000 for his share of the item.

Time passed, wounds healed, and Mrs. S regained her strength. Then, she decided to sell the rug, hoping to recoup some of her investment. She began with the store where it had been purchased. Their response was a resounding "No takebacks." Undeterred, she sought the expertise of an auctioneer to appraise the rug. The revelation was astonishing and disheartening—the appraised value was a mere $5,000.

Once considered a crown jewel of their opulent lifestyle, the rug was now reduced to a fraction of its original worth. The consequences reverberated throughout their divorce proceedings.

A valuable life lesson emerged through this cautionary tale of material possessions and their emotional entanglements. Mrs. S's impulsive purchase proved costly. The Aesop's fable or fortune cookie version: Hasty decisions may have far-reaching consequences.

The gap between the perceived value and the appraised worth revealed the arbitrary nature of monetary assessments. Art, after all, lies in the eye of the beholder. Its value is subjective—influenced by personal preferences, cultural contexts, and emotional connections—and extends beyond its monetary worth.

Should material abundance eclipse love, trust, and emotional fulfillment? Does our mania to amplify external appearances close our eyes to the effect our life choices have on others?

The S family rug made me hit the pause button. How should I evaluate, reevaluate, and question my perception of value for my clients? While some objects require evaluations, a class of objects defy conventional appraisal methodologies and transcend the confines of monetary value. No price tag or appraisal can capture the essence of their value, for they are priceless in the chapters of our personal histories—their worth lies in our hearts.

When I first met Mrs. L, she greeted me in her Riverside Drive apartment doorway with skepticism and biting humor, making it clear that she expected me to prove my worth. I immediately connected with her feistiness and admired her quick wit. She missed her late husband and their shared memories of watching sunsets over New Jersey from their tiny porch. He had immortalized that image by painting it on their closet doors—a touching reminder of their special place and time in a bygone New York City.

Mrs. L, with her fierce independence and vibrant spirit, held onto the memories of her life in the city with her beloved partner. As I began working on her downsizing project, I couldn't help but be moved by her story and the contrast those doors presented to the tale of Mr. and Mrs. S's expensive yet undervalued rug.

Despite Mrs. L's resistance to leaving her space, the reality of her declining health necessitated a major change. Her daughter, a professor in Eugene, Oregon, had found a suitable facility for her, but Mrs. L had one condition: She didn't want to be surrounded by what she called "annoying old people." Her discerning taste and appreciation for the arts, particularly opera, shone through as she shared stories of witnessing performances by legendary artists from Ezio Pinza to Leontyne Price.

The impending move left Mrs. L devastated, knowing that the new owners would discard the closet doors and, with them, her husband's most significant memento. Sensing her attachment to the doors, my team and I devised a creative solution. My project manager captured a photograph of them, and, using the very best of modern technology, we had the image printed onto a quilt. It was a snapshot of her life in New York and her relationship with her husband; she could quite literally wrap herself up in those priceless memories.

I'll never forget the gratitude and joy expressed in her voicemail thanking us for that quilt. It reminded me never to overlook the emotional weight that objects can carry and the importance of preserving and honoring our stories. Through these stories, I have come to understand that the value we assign to our possessions goes beyond their price tags; it's the emotional connection they foster and the experiences they represent.

It is through understanding and embracing this truth that we can find peace and harmony in our spaces.

1970: Grandpa and Grandma Ditchman, my dad, and Grandma Schultz.

With my fur brother, Charlie, in 1971.

With Grandma Schultz in Ohio, 1972.

Christmas with Daddy, 1979.

At work with Mom, 1981.

With Daddy, 1981.

"Charlie's Angels" hair, 1983.

Daddy's last birthday, 1984.

Family at Grandpa's funeral, 1992.

With my precious Tommy in Hawai'i, 1992.

Living in Turkey, 1996.

With Mom, 1997.

With Julie somewhere in India, 1997.

Thailand, 1997.

Our dining room at 115 Central Park West.

The apartment on John Street, 1999.

September 11, 2001.

Wedding Day surrounded by Seriatim Team: Shannon, Jennifer, Nicole, and Heather, 2003.

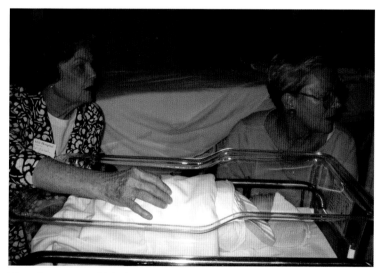

BB and my mom with baby Bev, 2004.

Proud parents, 2004.

Panchali and baby Bev, 2005.

Bev and Joyce, 2006.

Finn, 2020.

CHAPTER 8

Bringing My Work Home

Each time I pass by Hotel des Artistes on West 67th Street, my thoughts drift to a client who, despite never meeting him, left an indelible mark on my understanding of life. An heir to an Oklahoma oil fortune, he reveled in the carefree opulence of his residence at this prestigious address. His youthful years were spent in lavish indulgence. With his apartment solely in his name, he embarked on extended vacations to exquisite destinations across the globe. This whirlwind lifestyle abruptly ended with an untimely demise—a tragic consequence of a drug overdose in Paris.

In the wake of their son's passing, his devastated parents sought my assistance through an attorney. Tasked with managing a complex and contentious estate, he disclosed: "There's a considerable amount of wealth at stake, yet he left no will. We require thorough cataloging, inventorying, and storage of the apartment's contents in Oklahoma City." To this day, those possessions remain in storage.

The recurring monthly bills serve as persistent triggers, invoking the anguish and heartache of the son's premature passing. Despite his family's abundant resources and support, these crucial tasks go unresolved, leaving them to grapple with the aftermath.

Furthermore, what becomes of the potted plants, the pricey cutting board, the silly trinkets, the photo albums, the soccer trophies, and the sentimental family heirlooms? Who attends to these possessions? Where lies the reverence for these memories?

And how does a professional move manager learn from her clients' missteps? Can we succeed in helping our own families in their endeavors? At that juncture, listening wanes, understanding falters, and clarity dissipates.

Our move out of the Majestic, my childhood home, came about during a perfect storm of unpleasant events. The Global Financial Crisis, or Great Recession, had been brewing for years and became front-page news in late September 2008. The effect on our stocks and other investments was catastrophic. New York is America's financial epicenter, and its inhabitants were among the first to feel the impact of the fallout. Many families, including mine, were changed irrevocably and are still dealing with the aftermath.

Naturally, things got worse before they got better. The co-op raised the monthly maintenance fee, and we had no option but to list the apartment for sale. This part of my story is about upheaval. It turned me and my family upside down. If I had to pick one word to describe the feeling, it would be *relentless*.

As I look back on 2008 and '09, I still feel tremors. I remember the sickening feeling of watching the news, seeing the headlines, and talking about it over dinner sitting at the dining room table that would never again fit in our newer, smaller apartments. That twelve-foot-long table had been a zone of comfort and entertainment for all of us: every meal, every holiday and everyone had been invited to gather there. Our front door was always open, with an extra bed. I had traveled to Hawai'i, Southeast Asia, and Turkey, knowing places would be there for me when I returned. I belonged there. My family belonged there. Or so I thought.

There were three moves in one. First, we had to deal with the loss of our beloved friend Barbara "BB" Brine. In May 2009, we relocated her from Central Park West to an assisted living facility in New England. The weight of the transition was palpable as Mom and I unpacked her belongings, attempting to create a semblance of familiarity in an unfamiliar place. But how could we truly settle her? She had left behind her cherished home and the life she had built in the bustling heart of New York City.

Just a few hours outside the city, the facility felt like a distant world. Aunt Josephine had done her best to adorn the space with beauty, but it couldn't replace BB's lost connections. She was severed from her New York City roots, her purpose dissipating as her memory began to fade.

BB's memory slipped away without the same engagement, without the company of her daily friends and the vibrant community she once knew, and she descended further into the abyss of dementia.

Eventually, she moved again to a facility in Rye, New York, specifically designed for those battling the disease. As I walked the dimly lit hallways, I couldn't help but feel the weight of the collective suffering. People were confined to chairs, their bodies restrained, and the echoes of their drooping spirits reverberated through the corridors. It was a heartrending sight, reminiscent of the haunting imagery in *One Flew Over the Cuckoo's Nest.*

BB was an integral part of our daily lives. As Mom and I approached her, we saw her head lift and her eyes move. Though she couldn't articulate her thoughts, her expression seemed to say, "Ah! I recognize you two." In that brief moment, a sense of peace enveloped us all. But it wasn't long after that encounter that she passed away, consumed by the relentless grip of Alzheimer's.

The insidious nature of the disease defies words. It silently erodes the very essence of a person, gradually extinguishing the light of their being. That last memory of BB lingers—the way her eyes moved, reflecting a flicker of recognition amidst the fading fragments of her mind. Yet, my actual memories of her are rooted in the warmth of our shared moments in the apartment.

Her decision to move from the Majestic had a profound impact, not just on her own life but on the course of my mother's as well. Her absence created a void that could never be filled, a reminder of the inevitable passage of time.

In professional organizing, I have encountered countless clients burdened by the weight of their personal stories, their pain seeping into my soul. It is a double-edged sword—the ability to empathize deeply with those I help and the challenge of carrying their burdens.

Mindfulness guru Jon Kabat-Zinn penned a notable book, *Wherever You Go, There You Are*. While the sentiment captured in the title is not novel, having likely been borrowed from ancient wisdom such as Confucius or even earlier sources, it has endured and been recycled throughout the ages. Though beneficial, the aphorism fails to acknowledge the transformative power of the journey itself.

Departing from the familiar abode where one's roots have been firmly planted is an extraordinary undertaking, requiring tremendous effort to bring it to fruition. Every step of the way, as you embark on your chosen path, countless decisions and inevitable missteps shape your experience, demanding your attention around the clock. And when you finally arrive at your intended destination, self-criticism creeps in, prompting you to ask questions like: *Why couldn't I have done better? Why didn't I handle it differently?*

I'm one of the country's experts on downsizing and relocating families and small businesses. I had done hundreds of projects, yet I've never felt more helpless, inept, or discombobulated. I knew it would be hard, but I was unprepared for the emotional and physical toll. The fabric that held my family together seemed to be unraveling. I've never felt more vulnerable and exposed.

As with any Seriatim project, we had to help the client put their best foot forward to sell the apartment. Despite the economic turbulence, we needed to invest in renovations, big and small. A broken lampshade here, a leaky drain there, new paint, carpet—everything had to be considered and reconsidered regarding aesthetic improvements. Mom called Josephine, who shipped furniture from California for staging purposes. We put most of our other things in storage.

I had to rely on my team when sorting, eliminating, and donating items. Mom could listen to them and hear what they were saying. They worked side by side with her to make many tough decisions. Instead of "Joyce, you need to get rid of these shoes," they'd say, "Out of these five pairs, maybe you can pick your four favorites?" During an organizing crisis, diplomacy is the only strategy.

My project manager Yasmine managed to do everything flawlessly. It was a great comfort. Pete was often traveling back then, and the planning and orchestrating of the move fell on me. That made me resentful and angry. It strained my marriage and my relationship with my family, for sure. I had seen it happen to clients, and I had always been the stable, clearheaded person in the room. Now I was the one feeling restless, agitated, and fussy. I was a mom, daughter, and wife, and, like so many women, I felt the weight of the project on my shoulders even though I had asked for help. It was a lot to handle emotionally.

After the apartment was listed, I couldn't face reality or deal with the situation. I took Bev to Racine, Wisconsin, to visit my friend Sandy and go horseback riding. I asked Pete to find an apartment we could live in and Mom could crash until we found her a place with a big enough kitchen. We rented a 900-square-foot apartment on West 112th Street near Ms. M's. I saw it the day we moved in. It was a brand-new building near the B/C line at 110th Street and relatively close to Bev's school on 89th Street between Columbus and Amsterdam Avenues.

We had to face the fact that the apartment would sell for less than we had hoped. Mom had been a broker for years, and I followed real estate trends as part of my daily work at Seriatim. Given the size of the space, the location, and the quality of the building, we knew we had a gem. Had it been during better times, we may have gotten twice as much. Closing was on August 17, 2010.

The new owners did a gut renovation. The table stayed in the apartment and was demolished along with whatever else. I shouldn't have let it go. I didn't fight for it. I should have asked for a remnant of it. I would have liked to have made a nightstand out of it or something sweet to remember the good times we had. I couldn't bear to watch it be destroyed. I was shell-shocked.

For me, the loss wasn't just a statistic for the monthly real estate market report. I had lost the place where my father, grandfather, and great-aunt had passed away. It was the first time I dealt with my father's death. We had to say goodbye to him. I could no longer be near his things and my memories of him. I couldn't retrace his footsteps or feel his presence. Everything—the whole city—felt like new territory. I think for Mom, too. Old ghosts, new fears, all at once. Some of it was on a conscious level, and other bits and pieces were nestled in the corners of my mind.

Here's where the story becomes noxious. Our stuff from the Financial District had been in storage with the mover since 2005. When the boxes were redelivered, I noticed they looked crinkled on the tops and around the edges. They weren't wet but looked like they had been wet and dried out. Then, I started taking things out. Moths! My Asian carpets, silk curtains, and upholstered furniture—all like Swiss cheese. The damp wool was like a petri dish. I ended up in the fetal position on the kitchen floor of our apartment at 112th Street, crying hysterically.

Everything that could go wrong actually did. I washed some items as best I could, but it was a lost cause. All those souvenirs and memories were ruined. I spent six months battling with my insurance company. They told me that infestation was not a claimable issue, then they reviewed the damages and determined that water was the actual cause, so they offered me a number just shy of $25,000.00.

Luckily, I knew how to make an inventory and keep date-stamped "before" pictures. Words to live by: Any inventory is better than no inventory. After many disagreeable phone calls, I was paid what they owed me: a little over $90,000.00, close to four times the amount of the insurance company's original proposal. It made me feel better but didn't fix the anxiety 2010 had brought me. It took us many years to recover from it.

The first few months were rough. My husband, daughter, and mom shared the nine-hundred-square-foot space. Oh, and we also had two rabbits. We were no longer able to retreat to our private areas. Remember, too, that I also lost my dedicated workspace. I had to set up my office in that tiny apartment. My project coordinator, Cherise, handled everything related to my business and personal life. At the same time, employees would come and go at all workweek hours. At the beginning of 2011, Mom got her place nearby, on Central Park North. My team and I had to revisit all those boxes from the Majestic. Indubitably, the most prolonged move I've ever had to manage was my own.

Nearly a year after selling my childhood home, Haas came into my life. We had an instantaneous connection. We're both only children, and we understand a lot about each other. He started working as my assistant and ran my office for many years. He was also with me when we decided nine-hundred square feet weren't enough. We talked it over every which way. Do we leave Manhattan and go to the 'burbs? Can we find something larger for around the same price we're paying now? As long as it's not Brooklyn or New Jersey, I said. The search for a suitable apartment began.

Bev was getting bigger and bigger and would enter middle school, which is every city parent's personal nightmare. We had also acquired a new pet: Lily the Frog, whose tank required bimonthly cleaning sessions. I had two choices: live with frog gunk in my kitchen or move somewhere with a slop sink. And we found one—in the ground-floor brownstone apartment on West 148th Street, where we stayed for ten years. We were delighted that Columbia Secondary School would serve as both middle and high school. Bev's friends could come over and make as much noise as they wanted in the basement. We also adopted a blind mutt named Finn, who positively stole my heart. (As this book comes to a close, Lily is still with us, too!)

Mom and me, well, we can laugh about all of this now. We emerged from the rubble stronger and surer of our bond. That's the wellness piece that I like to speak about to clients and business associates. Ultimately, the project was about my family's well-being. Pete and I are still together because the challenges were ours. We figured out how to face them together. Leaving apartment 2G taught me that I could learn to feel whole again in a different place. Now, even when the ground's uneven, I can stand securely on my own two feet.

CHAPTER 9

Prime Time

My longest and perhaps most rewarding job began in the summer of 2010. Mr. B was one of the most successful TV stars of the 1970s. After working on his estate intermittently for seven years, I came to know and understand the man behind the showbiz persona even though I never met him.

I wish I could have met him. He died in 2001, and his widow was diagnosed with Alzheimer's in 2009. Their daughter-in-law, Isabella, was made the estate executor shortly after that. She married into a family with the classic Hollywood story of addiction, drugs, disease, and endless distress. It took many years for her to find her voice. It was a privilege to accompany her on that journey.

I first met Isabella at an apartment in the West 70s, near my home at the Majestic. It was Mr. and Mrs. B's principal East Coast residence. After Mrs. B got sick, their family office encouraged Isabella to liquidate properties and assets. Her real estate broker gave her my name. The circumstances for their relocation weren't ideal. It was a time of frustration and anguish; decisions were made hastily. They relied on a put-it-all-in-storage approach: hundreds of boxes were shipped back to California or stowed in another New York City apartment. At first, it made my job easier. They were happy to get the apartment listed and sold so quickly. I thought my contribution was complete. Three years later, I got a call from Isabella. "Do you travel to California?" I hung up the phone and started packing my bag.

There were three houses in Los Angeles: one in Westwood, another in North Hollywood, and their primary address in Carbon Mesa. Before Mr. B died, they had also owned the house next door to that beach house. After it was sold, they sent boxes of contents to storage or transferred them to the adjacent house. Someone had to go through them and decide what to keep, donate, or throw away. That was one small portion of the brain teaser. Isabella was planning to care for Mrs. B at the Carbon Mesa home. Certain renovations were needed to accommodate a wheelchair and full-time caregivers.

Isabella was not only the executor of the estate but also the healthcare advocate and decision-maker. But which house was best to stay in during the renovation? Can Mrs. B go up and down stairs? Where should we move the bed? Where will the aide sleep? How far do they have to commute? Where's the doctor? They needed a long-term strategic plan.

Sonya Weisshappel

I never met Mrs. B, but I got to know her through her objects. She was born in Kansas of Native American heritage. Her grandfather had been a prominent photographer whose work depicted American Indians and their daily life on reservations. She kept his vital collection and helped edit a book of his life and work. Outstanding art and relics were present in nearly every room. Each item had to be inventoried and archived.

Additionally, we had to deal with her wardrobe and other personal items. What would we do with her fancy purses, hats, and shoes? She had been in the throes of illness for years and was completely bedbound. We cataloged everything and began a comprehensive donation list.

Isabella's husband had committed suicide after years of depression and drug abuse. Their son was only a baby when it happened. They had met while she was working on the wardrobe crew for one of Mr. B's television programs. Over the years, Isabella battled her addiction problems as well. Our time together was sometimes arduous but never contentious. She was a hard worker and would do her best to focus until she physically couldn't stand it.

I don't think Isabella ever felt accepted by the family. Yet, she had become responsible for their estate, legacy, and her son's financial future. It was an unenviable position. She knew she needed help and wasn't afraid to ask for it. Despite the difficult days and hours I may have spent managing the job, her grit and perseverance often surprised me.

The Carbon Mesa house had been their headquarters for parties and entertainment. It was astonishing. Isabella had her wedding on a private beach. Mrs. B's hospital bed had huge bay windows with unobstructed ocean views and a perfect sea breeze. When she died in 2014, Isabella's role as executor became more burdensome, and Seriatim's project became even more expansive. Ironically, it was not Isabella but rather her son who was the heir to the family's fortune.

The estate needed a total and proper value for many purposes, particularly from an insurance point of view. The Carbon Mesa house had ongoing issues with flooding and couldn't be placed on the market without wide-ranging repairs. There had also been minor break-in attempts at the home in Westwood. I also learned there was a "small" airplane hangar about an hour away that harbored Mr. B's vintage car collection, mostly Bentleys. I wondered: When was the last time art, cars, jewelry, and other valuables had been appraised? My work in the relocation industry has taught me a lot about insurance. I am confronted with questions about it every day, and I've helped clients address potential mistakes with their homeowner or renter's insurance and mover insurance.

Most people don't think about these things until it's time to move. I think you should reconsider your insurance yearly. In the case of Mr. B's family, I knew they were underinsured and overtaxed, but they didn't know how to deal with it because they were still grieving.

Priority number one: bring everything up-to-date, with no ifs, ands, or buts.

We began to declutter and inventory items that had been consolidated into the Carbon Mesa home. I planned to use that location as our central hub and staging ground for movers and other vendor appointments. Isabella had rented at least four storage units in the LA area. All of them needed to be cleared out and delivered to Carbon Mesa. Movers unpacked thousands of boxes and left items on the floor and other surfaces throughout the home. We sorted them by category—dishes, cookbooks, table linens, and lamps. These items needed to be unpacked, repacked, and redistributed.

Concurrently, we went through the boxes from New York that had yet to be opened. The project scope was much larger than I had anticipated and was becoming more and more unpredictable. My team member Kara and I flew to California and stayed for seven to ten days at a time. We'd sleep in guest rooms at one of the houses and drive to and from different locations. Los Angeles is all about driving.

Envelopes and loose papers appeared in every piece of furniture with a drawer or cubbyhole. I started making separate boxes for paperwork and lost count after I'd filled four hundred of them. It was clear that Mrs. B's affliction with Alzheimer's had been lurking for years. At one time, Mr. B's documents were mixed in with fan mail, press clippings and interviews, old headshots, junk mail, restaurant menus and flyers, VHS, and Betamax tapes.

I went through everything. I could tell they had been a power couple, a bonded pair. Isabella told me she was never the same after his death. All you had to do was read their love letters, and you know they were meant to be together.

Mr. B had tiny handwriting, very meticulous. He wrote in his journal daily, sometimes about the weather or a bullet-point list of his accomplishments. He had prepared or considered dozens of scripts and scribbled notes on every page, sometimes between each line of dialogue. He managed a theatre company in Los Angeles along with another notable stage and screen actor. He also wrote screenplays, short stories, and songs of his own. Not to mention the photographs of famous actors, writers, and politicians. It was a treasure trove.

The life insurance policies, keys to safe deposit boxes, and deeds concerning real estate investments were even more pressing. There were other documents related to the provenance of art that had been purchased years ago, but no one knew where it had gone. Isabella had authorized the insurance payments but didn't know if the pieces were still in the family's possession. We called the family office to discuss it. The lack of support we received was startling. "Don't bother. Just shred those papers," they said. I told them absolutely no way, no how. I wasn't interested in throwing anything away.

I created a fifteen-page document of loose ends they needed to investigate and clean up. Isabella hired a lawyer to assist her in communicating with the family office representatives. She accessed the safe deposit boxes and found tens of thousands of dollars worth of jewelry. I later found out that the insurance policies were alone worth $750,000. The family office never knew they existed.

Isabella and her son decided to liquidate almost everything, including the second New York City apartment, and start fresh at a new home in the Southeast. Managing that part of the project didn't require much traveling. We went through all the boxes from the old apartment, created a donation list, and the movers picked it up and delivered most of it to donation facilities. A few Warhols and other pieces of art were worth keeping. We flew back to California to prepare the other houses for the market. It was like peeling an onion, figuring out the layers. You have to trust that you'll get where you want to go eventually, even if you take some unexpected turns. We were able to get the Carbon Mesa house listed by the spring of 2015. It didn't sell until 2017. I sent most of Mr. B's archives to his alma mater, Mrs. B's art and her father's photographs to the Smithsonian.

Of course, I had it all appraised first. I kept their childhood memorabilia and wedding pictures. I wanted their grandson to know there were happier times and try to hold onto them. To paraphrase Einstein: "Imagination is often more powerful than knowledge." The same holds for how we imagine or interpret memories through photographs. A child or child-in-law may be unable to see and experience them without remembering more sorrowful times. But don't toss them in the garbage.

You never know how beneficial those images may be for future generations.

When the house sold, I realized I hadn't been prepping for a real estate closing; I was helping to finish a chapter of this family's life and watch them turn over a new leaf. Isabella and her son could finally start to make their own life. They moved to Tennessee and took Mr. B's favorite Bentley. Seven years, countless plane rides and takeout meals, calls home to ask how Bev was doing at school. I gave a large piece of myself to this one. The feeling of gratification did not come immediately; when it did, it was immeasurable.

CHAPTER 10

Flying the Coop

Ms. Q grew up on Annandale Avenue in Portsmouth, Rhode Island. I came to find out she was from the type of Old-Money people who are "House-Rich."

Here are my notes from her "Client Snapshot" in my database: "Not truthful about money; pays bills late; procrastinates; sometimes slips out the back door; uses parrot, Gustav, as an excuse for everything."

Ms. Q never wanted help, and she never stopped resisting. But she was in trouble, and she knew it. Her sister called me some time in 2011. Ms. Q had fallen in her Upper East Side home, and the bird was so stressed that he had plucked out his feathers. All three of her siblings were worried about her living alone and being vulnerable. They convinced her to sell her home on Sutton Place and rent an apartment in an assisted living facility on Riverside Drive.

Ms. Q had all the money in the world. She should have been the last to worry about finding proper care. On the contrary: It was a nightmare for her and her family.

The apartment was a duplex on the first two floors of a well-appointed building. Ms. Q had marvelous things, mostly family heirlooms—oil paintings, Persian rugs, first-edition books, and other high-end antiques she'd inherited from her "prior life." Other than that, I don't think she would mind me saying she was not gifted with a keen aesthetic eye. Her look was frumpy, and her clothing was typically one or two sizes too large. She was in her mid-70s, had never been married, and could be devilishly conniving in a somewhat endearing way. She loved a good game, whether it was Backgammon or a battle of wits, and read everything she could get her hands on. An avid news junkie, she would regularly incite not-so-friendly debates. No one would ever accuse her of being "mushy," but she was sporadically agreeable and sometimes pleasant—except when it came to money.

My assistant Haas said Ms. Q was "a Flannery O'Connor character lost in Yankeeville." She was a person with either intentional or unintentional incongruities: She kept her wet bar fully stocked even though she never entertained; she had no children but loved teaching; she had plenty of money but hadn't paid her taxes in years; she studied psychology but couldn't (or wouldn't) learn to communicate her emotions to others. She'd talk about her feelings roundaboutly, ironically via pet-parrot telepathy: "Gustav is tired today; he doesn't want to work," or "Gustav is nervous about tomorrow's appointment with the movers." So I'd say, "What does Gustav think we should do?" Her response: "I'll ask him."

I didn't hit the ball after the first bounce but I learned how to play her game. As a side note, Gustav had been the pet of one of Ms. Q's students. The child was diagnosed with a terminal illness and died. The family gifted Ms. Q the bird for whatever reason. It may or may not have been much more complicated. I think something happened that made her stop teaching. She either quit or was fired; it doesn't matter one way or the other. It was a disturbance, and the matter had been left unresolved. The bird was something good that came from it.

I realized that Ms. Q had many bruises that wouldn't heal. She was different from Panchali and even Mr. O. She didn't have piles of clothing or trash; she had no collections, not even a trinket or knickknack. Nonetheless, I am convinced that her emotional dilemmas originated from similar experiences in childhood or as a young adult. Those kinds of injuries require treatment and medication, but the pain never goes away. We soon found out that Ms. Q had been self-medicating.

I'll do my best to put the events of her relocation into chronological order. I managed three different moves for Ms. Q in less than two years. First, I'll speak about moving into the Manhattan assisted living facility. She opted for the biggest and the best penthouse apartment that was available. Most of the residents had one-bedroom units. Hers had two: one for her and one for Gustav. The rent was over $20,000 a month. One would have thought the services would be impeccable; they were, in reality, shockingly abhorrent.

The first misstep was the floorplan: no measurements! The rooms weren't even laid out correctly! It was useless. We tried our best to see what would fit and what wouldn't, then tagged the items Ms. Q could bring from Sutton Place. The rest went to auctions, donations, or other family members. (Except for one painting that was shipped to the Newport Historical Society.) Ms. Q became weary of us and escaped from the back door.

Once we got her in, the next obstacle was dealing with her twenty-four-hour care team. Ms. Q hated every single one of them. She didn't want them sitting on the sofa, watching her; she wanted a friend. I think that's what all people wish for, especially older adults. She craved connection like everyone else. Ms. Q was also a devotee of Chinese medicine: acupuncture, balms, oils, massages, etc. She said she had chronic pain but just wanted to be touched. Massages were a way for her to feel touch safely, to be stimulated without having to engage with sex or emotional attachment. It could also have been about power. Wouldn't we all get more massages if we had the free time and money to burn?

The facility was in a relatively old building, and the brick had to be repointed. The refurbishing crew had placed something on the rooftop to rig their equipment. Not long after Ms. Q moved in, her bedroom ceiling fell in. She was lying in bed when it happened. To make matters worse, it had been raining non-stop for weeks, and there was mold. She got an infection in her chest and had to be taken to the hospital. The resident care supervisor moved her into temporary quarters, a dark studio room, but they kept charging her the full rate. It was a dump. The appliances were out-of-date, and the storage space was pitiful. There was scarcely enough room for a vacuum cleaner.

The Seriatim team returned and took the elevator up and down from the penthouse, carrying as much as we could to help her get settled for a second time. Ms. Q was in and out of the hospital with her infection. While collecting some clothing and personal items, we discovered a drawer full of pill bottles—Oxycontin. I called a friend who's a geriatric care manager and asked her to drop what she was doing and get in a cab.

The penthouse apartment had to be repaired, which took many painful months. The apartment was still damp and smelled of mildew. It was challenging enough to convince Ms. Q to move there in the first place. Gustav's life was also disrupted: he was used to having free rein in the apartment and flying outside a cage. Ms. Q had these cardboard contraptions and indoor "gyms" to keep him active. While living in the studio, an aide opened the window on a spring day, and he flew out. Imagine Ms. Q's reaction. You might as well have taken one of her limbs! Fortuitously, a neighbor found him in a tree on West End Avenue, and he was returned safely to his mother.

Ms. Q was paying for and should have received white-glove treatment. They never even said, "We're so sorry. We'll make it up to you." Nothing. They were, in actuality, shameless victim blamers. The Q family could have sued them and made their lives hell. They had every right to do it, but they didn't. Ms. Q finally got fed up and moved out of that hellhole. She walked away like she was slipping out of the back door again.

A few months later, I got a phone call from Ms. Q while waiting for my plane to depart at LaGuardia. She had always kept odd hours and was a consummate night owl. She told me she was off Oxycontin and was thankful for what the Seriatim team had done for her. She said she was sorry if she offended me and added: "I love you." I told her I was never offended and loved her, too. And I meant it. When we first met, she was scared and alone and was at her most vulnerable. We brought her out of the trench. Sure, she could be brutal, but never nasty. I was able to help her because she let me in. I am thankful for the lessons she taught me.

We kept in touch for a long while. Ms. Q would even call me to complain about life, and I'd let her talk until she worked it out. She would also ask me to manage random tech snafus. One day, she called and said her brand-new iMac wasn't working. She said, "It's broken." It was a lovely day, and I asked Haas to come along.

When we arrived, Ms. Q said, "There's nothing he can do that I haven't already tried." As calmly as I could, I asked her, "Well, do you want to be right, or do you want it to work?" She replied, "Both!" Eventually, we figured out that the computer was connected to the power cord strip, but the strip wasn't plugged into the wall.

Even now, I want to pick her up in my arms and hug her. I loved being able to banter with her and to be able to call a spade a spade as they did back in her day. She was a kid at heart, a big kid. All she wanted was to be paid attention to, and we did that for her. She liked being doted on and the center of attention. She may have appeared combative or confrontational but was merely testing our boundaries. Even negative attention seems reasonable to a lonely person. I think I know why she never paid her taxes: She hoped someone would call her and she could fight with them. She wasn't looking for an adversary; she wanted a sparring partner. Would anyone rise to the occasion? No.

I think it all boils down to finding community— belonging. You don't always need friends, but you do need friendly faces and exchanges. Seniors may or may not have their wits about them. But they all face physical challenges at one time or another and need to be protected. For Ms. Q, I felt I could protect her, and in doing so, I could protect every family member or previous client I may have let down. Impossible, I know. Yet I persist.

CHAPTER 11

Boxed In

Sometimes a person's pain is so acute that there's no way to rescue them. That is one of the many hard lessons I learned from Mr. and Mrs. N. Their story unfolded like a tumultuous whirlpool of physical, mental, and emotional struggles, with their codependency serving as a toxic catalyst that spewed its venom onto anyone who entered their Manhattan apartment. For the Seriatim team, their case presented a paradox: Despite the simplicity of the task, creating and executing a project plan became a near-impossible feat.

On the page, the narrative was straightforward: a three-bedroom apartment on the Upper East Side, rendered unoccupiable by Mrs. N's debilitating illness; a flurry of third-party professionals, from real estate brokers to contractors, attempting to relocate them closer to her doctors; a temporary home, a New England summer retreat, and multiple off-site storage lockers; a litany of delays culminating in an eviction notice; and, to further complicate matters, a full-fledged shopping addiction that engulfed their lives, leaving us wading through unopened boxes, drowning in a sea of retail rubble.

One of my team members humorously compared the experience of organizing Mr. and Mrs. N. to whitewater rafting. Even minor complaints, distractions, or scheduling issues could send the entire operation cascading down treacherous waterfalls or smashing into unforgiving rocks, requiring us to start the next day anew. At one point, they began blaming my team and me for all their misfortunes, drawing us into an exhausting battle where there could never be a victor.

Even now, as I write this book and replay scenes in my head, aware that I did my best, a heavy sense of guilt lingers for having failed them. I've realized that there are limits to what organization and reshuffling can achieve when the underlying pain is so deeply rooted.

I first encountered Mr. and Mrs. N in the spring of 2017. Their desperation and hopelessness only intensified in the following years, exacerbated by the challenges imposed by the worldwide pandemic. Mrs. N was afflicted by a severe connective tissue disease that confined her to a bed or wheelchair. Ironically, her stubborn lack of flexibility spilled over into their project goals, hindering progress.

Her anger knew no boundaries, and she unleashed it upon her husband, my team, and anyone unfortunate enough to cross her path. If she managed to be cheeky, scornful, or merely sardonic, we considered it one of her better moods. Shopping provided her with a temporary dopamine fix, but once the boxes arrived, they joined the ever-growing pile of confusion and disarray.

She received close to 150 boxes in a month, causing their once spacious 2,500-square-foot apartment to feel positively cramped. The clothing purchases rarely matched her size, yet she fixated on their arrival. Somehow, she always remembered to click that buy button, perpetuating the flood of packages.

For her, shopping was more than mere escapism. It offered a connection to a community, a way to reach beyond the confines of her bed and four walls. The motivations behind compulsive buying or hoarding behaviors are rarely rooted in consumerism. Every collection is unique and highly personal, often arising from a cavernous craving for safety, nostalgia, or solidarity.

I once had a client with a year-round Christmas fetish, buying anything that reminded her of the joy and innocence of her favorite time of year. As the Christmas collection accumulated and reached the height of a light switch, it became evident that she was experiencing a hoarding disorder.

When couples exchange vows and promise to stand by their partners "in sickness and health," they rarely anticipate the grief that can accompany long-term illness—grief as shocking and life-altering as death, only extended and more protracted. Mr. and Mrs. N had been grappling with her illness since their forties, and they had reached a point where they no longer knew what to do, where to go, or even how to think. They were worn out, emotionally and physically.

Mr. N, too, became the primary target of his wife's verbal attacks. Managing their expectations became complex, leaving me wondering whether he was brave or cowardly, sincere or manipulative.

Despite paying bills on time and seemingly appreciating our services, Mr. N would go weeks without responding to our calls, texts, or emails—unanswered questions accumulated, mirroring the unopened parcels stacking up in their apartment. Then, out of nowhere, he would call and accuse us of abandonment at nine o'clock on a Sunday evening. Dealing with objects and possessions are my expertise; human dynamics and diplomacy are different challenges altogether, especially when it becomes clear that people in need will not accept the help.

One of the predicaments I encountered with Mrs. N was her belief that consignment stores would eagerly accept any of her excess clothing. She needed to comprehend the limitations and logistics involved. Consignment stores, particularly those in crowded cities, have finite space and strict criteria for the items they accept. It's more complex than just handing over a bag of clothes. Each piece needs to be carefully evaluated, photographed, and sometimes even inventoried in a specific manner to meet their requirements.

Many assume that donating clothes with the tags still attached automatically makes them more desirable and valuable to charitable organizations. The truth is that most organizations face overwhelming volumes of donated clothing and need more resources to handle the influx. They often have to be selective, focusing on items in demand or good condition. Like a car's rapid depreciation the moment it hits the road, clothing loses its value once it leaves the store.

As a professional organizer, my role sometimes goes beyond the physical act of organizing spaces. It delves into the depths of human emotions, requiring a sensitive symmetry of empathy and detachment. Each client's journey becomes intersected with mine as I witness their struggles, triumphs, and the invisible weight they carry. Sometimes the best we can do is offer support and understanding, even if we can't fix their underlying issues.

When faced with individuals like Mr. and Mrs. N, who grapple with hoarding disorders and the pandemonium that accompanies them, the true depths of my empathy are tested. Their pain became palpable; I found myself absorbing their burdens and anguish as if to lighten their load and offer solace where I could. It blurred the boundaries between my clients' experiences and my own. I decided we had to walk away.

It was an exhausting cycle of emotional outbursts, failed attempts at finding solutions, and the ever-growing mountain of unopened boxes. Mr. and Mrs. N clung to the hope that someday they would find a way out of the ruckus, whether through a miracle cure or a change in circumstances that seemed forever elusive.

The prospect of Mrs. N's eventual passing hovered over them like a specter. It was a complicated truth that they held silently within themselves, aware that her death might bring a release from the turmoil that had defined their lives for so long.

It was an empath's dilemma: In absorbing their pain, I risked losing sight of my well-being, becoming entangled in a web of emotions that threatened to cloud my judgment and impede my ability to guide them toward a healing path.

Nevertheless, this mysterious connection for those struggling with hoarding disorders is also a source of strength. It fuels my unwavering commitment to their well-being and provides the foundation upon which we build trust and forge a path forward. It compels me to explore the underlying causes of their attachment and approach each client with unshakable compassion and the belief in the human capacity for change.

CHAPTER 12

From Concealment to Clarity

D ivorce is not just a legal process; it's a disman-
tling of a shared history. It tests the limits of
patience, resilience, and understanding, leaving
some on the brink of collapse.

As a professional organizer, I've had a front-row seat
to the highs and lows of this tumultuous journey, witnessing the upheaval firsthand and learning the true power of
empathy. It's a topic that brings me business, but more
significantly, it brings me face-to-face with the complex
emotions and fiery conflicts that can erupt when lives
intertwine and then abruptly unravel.

And what about the hidden narratives behind their
objects? How does one help others contend with what to
keep, what to let go of, and how to heal amidst the remnants of a fractured union—and do so with compassion
and sensitivity? I find myself acting as a mediator, thera-
pist, and confidante, striving to create a harmonious environment for their transition.

Confessions of a Chaos Whisperer

Managing explosive personalities during divorce proceedings has been one of my most daunting challenges. One project stands out: a couple's bitter disputes, resentment, and seething anger had permeated every corner of their former living space and seeped into the fabric of the objects they fought over, concealed, pilfered, and ruthlessly demolished.

It all started in January 2020, before the world was engulfed in the grip of the pandemic. Ms. T and I had been acquaintances since high school, and our paths crossed once again when she reached out for assistance. Her childhood home, a grand five-story brownstone in Harlem, had become the epicenter of her emotional anarchy. The recent passing of her mother, a well-known psychiatrist, cast a shadow over the house, making it difficult for Ms. T to make decisions about its contents.

The circumstances surrounding Dr. T's death were painful and complex. After a long battle with drug and alcohol addiction, she passed away inside the house, leaving behind a bedroom that resembled a war zone. The police investigation, indicating an overdose, had left the room cordoned off, preventing us from accessing it until they concluded their inquiries. The burden of dealing with the aftermath of her mother's addiction and the memories it conjured weighed heavily on Ms. T's shoulders.

Amid this troublesome environment, I was faced with the challenge of helping Ms. T navigate an emotional minefield. Her parents' divorce had been contentious, leaving latent scars that still haunted her. Dealing with personal objects became a trigger, a reminder of the trauma she had endured. It became clear that the two women had had a love-hate relationship.

My role as an organizer went beyond mere decluttering; it involved skillfully treading the fine line between preserving memories and understanding the psychological impact of divorce on Ms. T's life.

One of the fundamental aspects of my job is helping individuals uncover the actual value of their possessions. People often overlook the significance of certain items, dismissing them as worthless clutter. I knew better.

As you delve deeper, you unearth literal hidden gems and lost treasures that hold both sentimental and financial value, proving that the true worth of objects often lies beneath the surface. Also, I was reminded not to judge books by their covers.

At Ms. T's childhood home, a seemingly ordinary closet, neglected and filled with a mishmash of items, held a surprising revelation. Amidst the clothes hangers, discarded appliances, and swimming noodles, we stumbled upon a green box with a rare, hand-printed copy of James Joyce's *Ulysses* from Shakespeare & Co. in Paris. This literary masterpiece, entangled in the battles of her parents' divorce, evoked a wave of emotions, reducing Ms. T to tears. Beneath the clutter and chaos, valuable pieces of history often lie waiting to be discovered.

One day my mother, Joyce, joined me in the project. Together, we began decluttering Dr. T's bedroom. Every corner of that room told a story: papers scattered everywhere, jewelry strewed about, bookcases overflowing with memories—there wasn't an empty surface. As we stood shoulder to shoulder, armed with black garbage bags, the weight of the room's history bore down on us. We could almost hear her heartfelt pleas for help.

With no overwhelming time constraints looming over us, we were able to provide the support and organization needed to alleviate the burden. We painstakingly sorted through books, clothes, and personal effects, piece by piece. With each item, we uncovered fragments of familial strife. It was an emotionally draining yet cathartic process.

As the pandemic raged, Ms. T and I moved forward; our bond grew stronger. The crisis brought forth unprecedented hurdles that required innovative thinking and adaptability. In the final moments of closing out her mom's estate, I understood the loneliness that accompanies being the sole heir. Settling the estate proved immensely convoluted, with numerous layers to peel back—deciding what to sell, donate, gift, or discard. Our services held great value, serving as a guiding light during her darkest times of grief.

In the aftermath of that transformative project and experience, I couldn't help but marvel at the far-reaching impact divorce can have on our relationships, identities, and the objects we hold dear. As an organizer, I bear witness to these traumas.

Dr. T's estate also served as a poignant reminder of the unwavering support and guidance I've received from my mother. Her invaluable presence and assistance throughout my life became even more apparent during the months and years of the pandemic. It reinforced the significance of having someone by your side during challenging times, and it fueled my determination to be that source of support for others.

EPILOGUE

Just Getting Started

Life is full of uncertainties, and while we cannot change or replay the events that shake us, we can normalize conversations around them. Life transitions such as retirement, downsizing, illness, and death don't have to be daunting. By engaging in an open dialogue, we may alleviate the burdens of planning and decision-making.

Let me offer you an example: Have you ever considered discussing with your loved ones the type of flowers they would prefer at their funeral? Addressing this in advance eliminates second-guessing and provides peace of mind when the time comes. Whenever possible, proactively plan and prepare.

Life is back up and running—or is it? During the pandemic, the topic of self-care became paramount. Some people drank too much, overate, or felt depressed, but I now realize it was a gift—a pressing of the reset button. I reflect on the past couple of years with gratitude and determination. Despite its hardships, the pandemic provided the inspiration and impetus to fulfill an almost impossible dream of writing a book. Things were still and quiet, and for the first time in my life, I felt I had the space I needed to do something next-to-impossible: to put stories down on a page rather than recount them verbally.

August 2022 to August 2023 has been a year of my own emotional and physical transitions. People talk about the joys of taking a child to college, but it is a form of loss. It's worth it in the end, but the logistics of getting them there and then facing the emptiness of the nest is a huge adjustment. Time feels different. Planning for the future becomes different.

Pete and I were lucky to have an opportunity to go on vacation in Greece with friends immediately following Bev's departure. I was reminded that the world is so large and my day-to-day problems are tiny.

When I moved to Westerly, Rhode Island, in April 2023, I began to concentrate on expanding Seriatim. I am moving away from working *in* my business to working *on* my business.

The question during the pandemic was: How can I embrace this changing world? The question now is: What are other opportunities for change that I have yet to see? Is it counterintuitive to leave New York City in order to grow a New York-based business?

I'll answer with another question: What were the small joys from everyday life that you missed after they were taken away from you in March 2020? Honor your self-care routine. You can work from home and be on call while walking the dog in the park. You can do a Zoom instead of an in-person meeting. It requires changing the way you think about boundaries. I like jumping into things and showing up—like arriving on a job site and improvising.

For my younger self, that would have been detrimental. Now, in my early 50s, I'm embracing asking for help, delegating tasks, and focusing on solutions that allow everyone to do their best work while also feeling best.

The solitude of an empty nest has allowed me to contemplate and delve into more significant concepts. How can I reach more people? How can I bring more goodness into the world? What's even possible? These questions harken back to the early days of my career when I undertook my first organizing projects, some of which I have shared in this book. I have immersed myself in every aspect of my business and clients' journeys, tirelessly protecting their possessions and guiding them through life's transitions.

Yet, upon reflection, I realize that I have sometimes afforded myself the same level of protection. I have always been "of service," an empath who readily extends a helping hand. But lately, I have had those pivotal moments of realization where I recognize the need to say "yes" to myself more often.

We now find ourselves in a brave new world where it is more crucial than ever to find ways to protect ourselves, our businesses, and our families. The pandemic has taught us the value of resilience, adaptability, and forward-thinking. As I look ahead, I am committed to continuing my journey as a businesswoman and organizing guru, employing the lessons learned during this global crisis.

I must be mindful of things like my mother and aunts and uncles getting older and making the most of my time with them. As I have explored in this book, estate planning isn't merely for older people. I will continue to foster conversations around life transitions, encouraging open dialogue and proactive planning to alleviate the burdens accompanying major transitions in people's lives. With every client, every speech, and every story shared, I will strive to make a positive impact and leave a lasting legacy of compassion, efficiency, and empowerment.

Through it all, I will know that we can adapt to unforeseen circumstances. We have learned the importance of connecting with others, supporting one another, and embracing change. I am filled with gratitude for the incredible team I have assembled. They are not just skilled professionals, but individuals who exude a genuine love for organizing. Together, we have built a community where the joy of working and collaborating with others is at the heart of what we do. From the moment we step into a client's space, we bring not only our expertise but also a shared passion for transforming chaos into order.

But it doesn't end there. Our community extends beyond our team. The relationships we have cultivated with our vendors are an integral part of our success. They are not just suppliers; they are trusted partners who share our values and commitment to excellence. We rely on them for their expertise, products, and services, knowing that they are invested in our collective success. This sense of camaraderie and interconnectedness is what sets us apart. It's the enjoyment we find in being around other people, supporting one another, and working together toward a common goal.

At Seriatim, we understand that organizing is not just about tidying up physical spaces; it's about fostering meaningful connections and creating a harmonious environment that inspires and uplifts. The power of organization can transform lives.

I am the Protector. The Mama Bear. The Advocate. The Fixer. The Traveler. The Storyteller. The Listener. The Organizer. The Guru.

I'm ready, world. *What's next?*

About the Author

S onya Weisshappel grew up in New York City, where she started her organizing and move management company, Seriatim Inc., in 1999. Proudly dyslexic, Sonya founded her business to avoid writing a resume. More than two decades later, she and her Seriatim team have earned themselves a reputation as consummate Chaos Whisperers. Sonya is an alumna of the University of Wisconsin at Madison and the Goldman Sachs 10,000 Small Businesses Program, a longtime member of the National Association of Senior Move Manager (NASMM), and served as president of the New York Council of Relocation Professionals (NYCORP).